ANNE OF GREEN GABLES

L. M. Montgomery

TECHNICAL DIRECTOR Maxwell Krohn
EDITORIAL DIRECTOR Justin Kestler
MANAGING EDITOR Ben Florman

SERIES EDITORS Boomie Aglietti, Justin Kestler
PRODUCTION Christian Lorentzen, Camille Murphy

WRITER Laura Li-Jing Mehlinger
EDITORS Karen Schrier, Emma Chastain

Copyright © 2002 by SparkNotes LLC

All rights reserved. No part of this book may be used or reproduced in any manner whatsoever without the written permission of the Publisher.

SPARKNOTES is a registered trademark of SparkNotes LLC.

This edition published by Spark Publishing

Spark Publishing
A Division of SparkNotes LLC
120 Fifth Avenue, 8th Floor
New York, NY 10011

Any book purchased without a cover is stolen property, reported as "unsold and destroyed" to the Publisher, who receives no payment for such "stripped books."

02 03 04 05 SN 9 8 7 6 5 4 3 2 1

Please send all comments and questions or report errors to feedback@sparknotes.com.

Library of Congress information available upon request

Printed and bound in the United States

RRD-C

ISBN 1-58663-470-4

Introduction: Stopping to Buy Sparknotes on a Snowy Evening

Whose words these are you *think* you know.
Your paper's due tomorrow, though;
We're glad to see you stopping here
To get some help before you go.

Lost your course? You'll find it here.
Face tests and essays without fear.
Between the words, good grades at stake:
Get great results throughout the year.

Once school bells caused your heart to quake
As teachers circled each mistake.
Use SparkNotes and no longer weep,
Ace every single test you take.

Yes, books are lovely, dark, and deep,
But only what you grasp you keep,
With hours to go before you sleep,
With hours to go before you sleep.

Contents

CONTEXT	1
PLOT OVERVIEW	3
CHARACTER LIST	5
ANALYSIS OF MAJOR CHARACTERS	9
ANNE SHIRLEY	9
MARILLA CUTHBERT	9
MATTHEW CUTHBERT	10
THEMES, MOTIFS & SYMBOLS	11
THE CONFLICT BETWEEN	
IMAGINATION AND SOCIAL EXPECTATIONS	11
SENTIMENTALITY VERSUS EMOTION	11
FASHION CONCERNS	12
IMAGES OF NATURE	13
ANNE'S RED HAIR	13
THE LIGHT FROM DIANA'S WINDOW	14
SUMMARY & ANALYSIS	15
CHAPTERS 1–4	15
CHAPTERS 5–8	19
CHAPTERS 9–12	21
CHAPTERS 13–16	27
CHAPTERS 17–20	32
CHAPTERS 21–24	35
CHAPTERS 25–28	38
CHAPTERS 29–32	42
CHAPTERS 33–36	45
CHAPTERS 37–38	49

IMPORTANT QUOTATIONS EXPLAINED	53
KEY FACTS	59
STUDY QUESTIONS & ESSAY TOPICS	61
REVIEW & RESOURCES	65
QUIZ	65
SUGGESTIONS FOR FURTHER READING	70

Context

Lucy Maud Montgomery, known as Maud, was born in Clifton, Prince Edward Island, Canada, in November 1874. Her mother died when Montgomery was almost two years old. Her father remarried, and Montgomery spent her childhood with her grandparents in Cavendish, Prince Edward Island. In 1911, she married Reverend Ewen Macdonald and moved to Leaskdale, Ontario, where she raised three children before moving with her family to Norval, Ontario, in 1926. Montgomery died in Toronto in 1942 and is buried in Cavendish.

As a child, Montgomery read as much as she could. At that time, novels were considered inappropriate reading material for children. In an article titled "The Story of My Career," Montgomery wrote that the only novels kept in her grandparents' house were *Rob Roy* by Sir Walter Scott, *The Pickwick Papers* by Charles Dickens, and *Zanoni* by Edward Bulwer-Lytton. She had unrestricted access to poetry, however, and reveled in the works of such English poets as John Milton and Lord Byron. This early immersion in poetry likely influenced Montgomery's writing style, which is poetic and descriptive. Montgomery recalls the day she wrote her first poem, at age nine. Her father happened to visit her that day, and when she read the poem to him, he said unenthusiastically that the unrhymed lines did not sound much like poetry. Montgomery persevered despite his lukewarm reception; a few years later she published a poem in a local newspaper.

By the time she married at age thirty-seven, Montgomery had already established herself as an author. She kept a notebook in which she jotted down plots as they occurred to her, and while looking through this notebook, she found the following idea: "Elderly couple apply to orphan asylum for a boy. By mistake a girl is sent them." From these fragments, Montgomery concocted her first novel, *Anne of Green Gables*, which was published in 1908.

Historical and geographical setting plays a significant role in *Anne of Green Gables*. Several times, characters voice their Canadian pride, often in ways that modern audiences might find old-fashioned or even offensive. Mrs. Rachel Lynde, the most politically inclined character, espouses the ideas of the Liberal Party, which argued for a decentralized Canadian government that would preserve autonomy in the Canadian provinces. She and Marilla Cuthbert voice their distrust of foreigners and Catholics. Apart from politics, geography influences the pastoral world in which Anne lives. Many of the places in the fictional town of Avonlea come from Montgomery's childhood in Cavendish. Montgomery loved the beauty of Prince Edward Island, and Anne, like her creator, has a passionate attachment to nature and finds comfort in the outdoors when her family life torments her.

Anne of Green Gables marked the beginning of Montgomery's prolific writing career and the first in a succession of novels centered on young, adventurous female protagonists. After the success of *Anne of Green Gables*, Montgomery went on to write seven more novels about Anne, following the protagonist through adulthood and motherhood. Several novels in the Anne series have been adapted and made into a successful television miniseries. Montgomery's work has been translated into several languages, and Montgomery museums, plays, and houses on Prince Edward Island draw international visitors.

Plot Overview

MATTHEW AND MARILLA CUTHBERT are unmarried siblings who live on their ancestral farm, Green Gables, in the quiet town of Avonlea in Prince Edward Island, Canada. Matthew is sixty, and since he is getting too old to handle the farm work on his own, the Cuthberts decide to adopt an orphan boy to help him. This decision shocks the town gossip, Mrs. Rachel Lynde, who does not think Matthew and Marilla fit to raise a child.

Matthew, who is terrified of women, arrives at the train station and finds a girl orphan instead of a boy; the orphanage sent the eleven-year-old Anne Shirley by mistake. Anne's talkativeness and spirit charm Matthew, who shyly tells Marilla that he wants to keep her. Marilla hesitates at first, but after a trial period, she agrees to let Anne stay on.

Anne is a talkative and happy girl despite living an impoverished life as an orphan. Though she lacks social graces and education, she has a rich and sophisticated fantasy life and an optimistic and generous spirit. Because Anne acts according to her instincts and not according to a code of manners, she unintentionally defies expectations of proper ladylike behavior. She attends church for the first time wearing a wreath of wildflowers, for example, and screams at Mrs. Rachel for making fun of her red hair. Anne tries hard to oblige Marilla and follow her rules of social conduct, but she makes many mistakes, using liniment instead of vanilla in a cake, letting a mouse drown in the plum-pudding sauce, and delivering a heartfelt but ridiculous prayer on her first attempt to pray before bed.

Anne never had real friends before living at Green Gables, so she was forced to invent imaginary playmates. In Avonlea, she meets Diana Barry, a neighbor who quickly becomes her bosom friend. One afternoon Anne invites Diana to tea and accidentally gives her red currant wine instead of nonalcoholic raspberry cordial. Diana returns home drunk, and Diana's mother, thinking Anne has intoxicated Diana on purpose, forbids the girls to speak. The agonizing period of estrangement lasts until Anne saves Diana's sister, who is sick with the croup, which causes Mrs. Barry to forgive her.

At school, Anne feuds with a handsome, smart boy named Gilbert Blythe. When they first meet, Gilbert taunts Anne by calling her

Carrots and pulling her red braid. Anne is extremely sensitive about her red hair, and Gilbert's teasing infuriates her. She screams at him and smashes a slate over his head. This incident marks the beginning of a rivalry between Anne and Gilbert, the two smartest pupils, which lasts until the end of the novel.

As Anne grows up, she loses some of her childish flare for the melodramatic and romantic, and turns her spirited attentions to academics. A beloved teacher, Miss Stacy, recognizes Anne's intelligence and encourages her to join a special group of students preparing for the entrance exam to Queen's Academy. Her long-standing competition with Gilbert Blythe changes to an affectionate and familiar rivalry when, after four years of mutual silence, they both go to Queen's Academy. Striving to make Matthew and Marilla proud, Anne devotes herself to her studies wholeheartedly and earns the prestigious Avery Scholarship, which grants her enough money to attend a four-year college the following fall.

Thrilled by her future prospects, Anne goes home to Green Gables. Matthew, who has been having heart trouble, dies of a heart attack. When Anne learns that Marilla is likely to go blind, she decides to stay at Green Gables and teach nearby so that she can care for Marilla, giving up her aspirations for a four-year degree. Gilbert hears of her decision and gives up his post as the teacher at Avonlea school so that Anne can teach there and be closer to Marilla. After five years of rivalry, Gilbert and Anne forge a close friendship. Though her future path has narrowed considerably, Anne remains eternally optimistic and thinks cheerfully about her future.

Character List

Anne Shirley The protagonist of the novel. Anne is an orphan who is adopted by Matthew and Marilla Cuthbert and grows up on their farm, Green Gables. The novel follows Anne as she makes social blunders and tries to quickly absorb the rules of social conduct, religion, and morality that other children have grown up learning. She has difficulty mixing these social customs with her own unique sensibilities. Anne is stubborn, passionate, loyal, and intelligent. She loves beauty and fantasy, and wants to be a good person.

Marilla Cuthbert An unmarried woman who raises Anne. Marilla lives at Green Gables with her unmarried brother, Matthew. Marilla is all angles and straight lines, with a stern face and tightly knotted hair. This physical severity mirrors her moral and emotional severity. Although Marilla does not usually express emotion, underneath she has a wry sense of humor and a loving heart. Although she raises Anne strictly, she loves her adopted daughter, and by the end of the novel she has become softer and more expressive.

Matthew Cuthbert A sixty-year-old bachelor who lives at Green Gables with his sister, Marilla. Matthew is painfully shy and a little eccentric. Although he is terrified of women, he instantly likes Anne and pressures Marilla to adopt her. Anne considers Matthew a kindred spirit and always turns to him when she wants a sympathetic ear.

Diana Barry Anne's best friend. Diana is a plump, pretty girl Anne's age who lives next door to Green Gables at Orchard Slope. Diana and Anne become bosom friends immediately after they meet. Full of romantic notions about love and friendship, they swear devotion to each other forever. Although an agreeable girl, she lacks Anne's imagination, intelligence, and independence.

Gilbert Blythe A handsome, smart Avonlea boy who becomes Anne's rival when he makes the mistake of teasing her about her red hair. Anne swears never to speak to Gilbert, and even when he rescues her from the river, she refuses to break the silence between them. Anne's rivalry with Gilbert keeps her motivated throughout her academic career. By the end of the novel, the rivalry has become affectionate, and Anne and Gilbert have become friends.

Mrs. Rachel Lynde The town busybody. Mrs. Rachel likes nothing better than to give her opinion and preach morals. She lives next door to Green Gables with her meek husband, Thomas, and an affectionate, quarrelsome friendship exists between her and Marilla. Mrs. Rachel is outspoken about everything from politics to fashion, and, although childless, she never fails to advise Marilla on how to raise Anne.

Miss Muriel Stacy Anne's teacher. Miss Stacy becomes the Avonlea schoolteacher after the unpopular Mr. Phillips departs. Her unorthodox, liberal teaching methods worry the conservative Avonlea trustees and Mrs. Rachel, but all of her students love her. She is a role model and mentor for Anne.

Mrs. Allan Wife of the new minister, Mr. Allan. Anne admires Mrs. Allan for her youth, beauty, and natural goodness, and frequently turns to her for guidance.

Mr. Allan The new minister of Avonlea. Mr. Allan is a good man and a natural leader of the community. He and his wife, Mrs. Allan, earn the universal approval of the town.

Mrs. Barry Diana's mother. Mrs. Barry is a severe, unforgiving woman. She expects her children to follow strict and sometimes unreasonable rules and is quick to condemn Anne when Anne makes mistakes.

ANNE OF GREEN GABLES 7

Aunt Josephine Diana's old aunt. Aunt Josephine is very rich and lives in a mansion in the town of Charlotteville. She has come to expect people to cater to her, although when they do it bores her. Anne's vivacity and unorthodoxy charm Aunt Josephine, and she often invites Anne to visit.

Minnie May Diana's little sister. Minnie May is an important character mainly for the role she plays in reviving Anne and Diana's friendship. When Minnie May falls ill with the croup, Anne saves her life. As a result, Mrs. Barry gains a new respect for Anne and permits Diana to reestablish her friendship with Anne.

Ruby Gillis One of the youngest of the many Gillis girls. Ruby has learned about growing up from her older sisters, and loves to share her superior knowledge with Anne and their other friends. Ruby inclines toward sentimentality and hysterical fits. She cares more for her good looks and her string of boyfriends than she does for her studies.

Josie Pye A member of the notorious Pye family. Josie lives up to her family's bad reputation and inspires the dislike of her classmates. Anne tries to cultivate charitable feelings toward Josie but cannot manage to do so.

Jane Andrews A plain, sensible girl in Anne's group of friends. Jane is not particularly ambitious, imaginative, or pretty, but she is steadfast and reliable.

Charlie Sloane One of the first people to recognize Anne's charms. Charlie admires Anne from afar from the time they are children.

Moody Spurgeon MacPherson One of the boys in Anne's class at the Avonlea school and a classmate of hers at Queen's Academy.

CHARACTER LIST

Mr. Phillips The schoolmaster at Avonlea during Anne's first year at Green Gables. Mr. Phillips is an inattentive teacher and a capricious disciplinarian. Mr. Phillips spends class time flirting with his oldest student, Prissy Andrews.

Prissy Andrews A classmate of Anne's. Prissy, sixteen years old when Anne begins her studies at Avonlea School, is considered grown up enough to court the teacher, Mr. Phillips.

Mrs. Thomas Anne's first foster parent. Anne describes Mrs. Thomas as harsh and unkind. After the death of her alcoholic husband, Mrs. Thomas gives Anne up.

Mrs. Hammond Anne's second foster parent. Mrs. Hammond uses Anne as a maid and makes her care for her three sets of twins.

Mrs. Peter Blewett A woman living in Avonlea. Mrs. Blewett offers to take Anne in as a babysitter when she learns that Marilla intends to get a boy orphan in Anne's place. Marilla decides to keep Anne because Mrs. Blewett is a nasty, stingy woman, and not fit to care for a child.

Mr. Bell The church superintendent. Mr. Bell leads prayer every Sunday. Anne cannot stand his prayers because she finds them unimpassioned and boring.

Mr. Bentley A minister at Avonlea. Mr. Bentley does little to inspire his congregation and gives dull, lengthy sermons.

John Blythe Gilbert's father. Mr. Blythe courted Marilla when they were younger, but ended up marrying someone else. Marilla confides in Anne that she regrets ending her courtship with Mr. Blythe.

Mrs. Spencer A worker at the asylum where Anne lived. Mrs. Spencer brings Anne to Matthew and Marilla instead of the boy orphan they requested.

Analysis of Major Characters

Anne Shirley

When Anne arrives in Avonlea, she is a stray waif with a pitiable past, but she quickly establishes herself in Green Gables and the Avonlea community. She is not useful to Matthew and Marilla, her guardians, who wanted a boy orphan to help out on the farm. Still, Anne's spirit brings vitality to the narrow, severe atmosphere at Green Gables. Her desire for beauty, imagination, and goodness motivates her behavior. Although some people, like Matthew, recognize Anne's admirable qualities from the beginning, others misunderstand Anne and think her unorthodox behavior evidence of immorality. The very traits that make Anne unique and enrich her inner life also cause her to act passionately and stubbornly and to bungle chores. Reveries and daydreams constantly absorb her, taking up attention that Marilla feels should be spent thinking of decorum and duty.

As a child, Anne loves and hates with equal fervor. She makes life-long alliances with people she considers kindred spirits and holds years-long grudges against people who cross her. Anne's terrible temper flares at minimal provocations, and she screams and stamps her foot when anger overtakes her. Anne lusts for riches and elegance. She despises her red hair and longs for smooth ivory skin and golden hair. She imagines that which displeases her as different than what it is, dreaming up a more perfect world. As she grows older, Anne mellows. Her temper improves, she ceases to hate her looks, she appreciates the simplicity of her life and prefers it to riches, and although her imagination still serves her well, she loves the world as it is.

Marilla Cuthbert

Marilla begins the novel a sharp, severe woman. Only a faint sense of humor lightens her severity; with Mrs. Rachel and Matthew, Marilla allows her biting wit to peep through her propriety. At first, Marilla's narrowness and rigidity clash with Anne's romanticism and imagination. Marilla scolds Anne for her unusual behavior, criticizing her when she screams at Mrs. Rachel or decorates her hat with flowers. Marilla is an equally harsh ruler of her own thoughts and behavior. When she finds herself agreeing with Anne's candid, indecorous thoughts, she sternly rebukes herself. Marilla leads a rigid emotional life too. She rarely expresses her love for Anne, and when she does feel rushes of affection, she quickly stifles them.

Marilla's love for Anne is evident in her kind, fair treatment of her adopted daughter. Even her strict rules show Anne that Marilla cares for her and wants her to grow up well behaved and successful. Anne's unconventional ways interest Marilla as much as they shock her, and she must often suppress laughter at Anne's outrageousness to give Anne the scolding she deserves. Marilla softens gradually until she is able to tell Anne she loves her and can confide in her, confessing her own romantic travails as a young girl. She becomes able to express emotion more openly and voice her pride in Anne's successes.

Matthew Cuthbert

At the age of sixty, Matthew is known as a strange, timid man. His painful shyness becomes paralyzing when he is forced to interact with women, and he spends most of his time away from people, working the land at Green Gables. Despite Matthew's extreme shyness, Anne immediately appeals to him and sets him at ease. From the beginning, Matthew advocates for Anne. He expresses pride in all she does and seizes every opportunity to spoil her. Although when they adopt Anne Marilla makes Matthew promise not to interfere with the raising of the child, Matthew becomes increasingly involved in parental duties, especially when he feels Marilla is treating Anne too harshly. With his gentle persistence, he often wears away at Marilla until she agrees to let him and Anne have their way.

Whereas Anne and Marilla butt heads for years, Anne and Matthew instantly understand one another, and Anne listens to Matthew when no one else's arguments can sway her. She recognizes him as a "kindred spirit" and confides in him when she wants a sympathetic ear. In contrast to Marilla's manly severity and difficulty expressing emotion, Matthew exhibits motherly qualities. He openly tells Anne of his affection for her and pride in her, and he wants her to look pretty and feel comfortable with her friends. More gentle than Marilla, Matthew treats Anne with unflagging kindness. Anne influences Matthew positively; he loves her bright presence at Green Gables and becomes more outgoing and happier after she arrives.

Themes, Motifs & Symbols

Themes

Themes are the fundamental and often universal ideas explored in a literary work.

The Conflict Between Imagination and Social Expectations

Anne is guided by her imagination and romanticism, which often lead her astray. Daydreams constantly interrupt her chores and conversations, pulling her away from reality and into her own imaginary world. This escape pleases Anne, but her rich inner life often comes into conflict with Avonlea's expectations of appropriate behavior. Anne's imaginative excursions lead to everything from minor household disasters, such as baking an inedible cake, to life-threatening calamities, such as nearly drowning in an attempt to act out a poem. Marilla does not indulge in fantasy, and equates goodness with decorum and sensible behavior. She adheres to the social code that guides the actions of well-behaved ladies. Anne has difficulty understanding why Marilla doesn't use her imagination to improve upon the world. Partly Marilla is not naturally inclined to imaginativeness, and partly she worries for Anne, thinking that Anne will imagine and long for wonderful things and then experience painful disappointment when reality does not live up to her expectations. Anne wants to please Marilla by acting obedient and deferential, but she finds irresistible pleasure in her wild fantasies. As she matures, however, Anne curbs her extreme romanticism and finds a compromise between imagination and respectability.

Sentimentality versus Emotion

Anne's feelings run deep; she loves and hates with passion, and dreams with spirit. However, as a child, she cannot distinguish between true emotion and mere sentimentality, or fake emotion, often allowing herself to indulge in sentiment because she thinks it romantic. Her weakness for sentiment colors her fictional stories, which feature melodrama, true love, eternal devotion, and tragic loss. She and her friends enjoy histrionic displays of emotion, working up a weepy farewell to Mr. Phillips even though they dislike him and terrifying themselves by imagining the woods to be haunted.

In part, Anne's attachment to sentimentality provides a refuge from the real emotions of fear and loss she experienced as a child. Her parents' death left her at the mercy of others, and as a young girl she was treated not with the love and attention that most children receive, but with cruelty and carelessness. Because Anne knows the pain of real emotion, the play-world of sentiment is comforting to her. When she imagines sentimental stories and games, she is able to control the situation, as she could not in her dealings with real emotion. Only when Anne becomes an adult can she deal with real emotion. When Matthew dies at the end of the novel, Anne experiences real loss. As a well-adjusted woman, she can cope with the loss of someone dear to her and recognize her pain as real emotion, not the sentimental fluff of her childhood games.

MOTIFS

Motifs are recurring structures, contrasts, or literary devices that can help to develop and inform the text's major themes.

FASHION CONCERNS

Although fashion interests Anne because she wants to look pretty, she wants to be fashionable mainly because she believes being good would be easier if she were well dressed and beautiful. For Anne, fashionable dress overlaps with morality. She feels she would be more grateful if her looks improved and says she cannot appreciate God because he made her so homely. Anne also views fashion as a means of fitting into her group of friends. Her increasingly stylish clothes represent her transformation from humble orphan to schoolgirl to successful scholar and woman. When Anne arrives at Green Gables, she wears ugly skimpy clothes from the orphanage, which represent her loneliness and neglect. At Green Gables, Marilla initially makes Anne sensible dresses devoid of frills or beauty. A few years later, Matthew buys Anne a stylish dress with puffed sleeves. Eventually, even Marilla agrees to allow Anne fashionable clothes. The gradual acceptance of Anne's desire for fashionable clothes demonstrates the gradual shift of Matthew and Marilla's feelings for Anne. At first, Marilla feels kindly toward

Anne but does not see any reason to indulge her. Although Matthew would love to spoil Anne, he dares not speak against Marilla. Eventually, Matthew finds the courage to defy Marilla and give Anne a lovely dress, and Marilla comes to love Anne like a daughter and see the appeal of dressing her in fashionable clothes.

Images of Nature

Anne's powerful imagination reveals itself during her first ride to Green Gables, when she talks romantically about the beautiful trees and natural sights of Avonlea. Nature not only pleases Anne's eye, it gives her reliable companionship. She has lacked human friends and finds companions in plants and playmates in brooks. On her first night in Avonlea, when she fears no one will come for her, she takes comfort in the idea that she can climb into the arms of a tree and sleep there. For Anne, Avonlea, with its healthy trees, represents a pastoral heaven that contrasts with the sickly trees and coldness of her days at the orphan asylum. At Green Gables, she shows her respect for nature by giving lakes and lanes flowery, dramatic names. As she matures, she continues to love nature. During the stressful exam period at Queen's Academy, her love of nature relaxes her and helps her to remember what is truly important in life. At the end of the novel, she looks to nature as a metaphor for her future: full of beauty, promise, and mystery.

Symbols

Symbols are objects, characters, figures, or colors used to represent abstract ideas or concepts.

Anne's Red Hair

Anne's red hair symbolizes her attitude toward herself, which changes as the novel progresses. Initially, Anne hates her red hair. She thinks it a blight on her life and complains about it at every opportunity. Her loathing for her hair reveals her dislike of herself. No one has ever loved Anne properly, and she does not approve of her own mistakes and bad behavior. Later, Anne's acceptance and fondness for her red hair symbolizes her acceptance of herself.

The Light from Diana's Window

Anne looks to the light from Diana's window as a symbol of their eternal friendship. It is a familiar sight that gives Anne comfort at the end of the novel when she decides to stay in Avonlea and care for Marilla. Seeing the symbol of her loving friendship with Diana makes Anne feel better about sacrificing her ambition in order to do what she feels is the right thing.

Summary & Analysis

Chapters 1–4

Summary—Chapter 1:
Mrs. Rachel Lynde Is Surprised

> *Isn't it splendid to think of all the things there are to find out about? It just makes me feel glad to be alive.*
> (See QUOTATIONS, p. 53)

Mrs. Rachel Lynde, the town busybody, lives with her meek husband on the main road of Avonlea, a small rural town in Prince Edward Island in Canada. Mrs. Rachel, as she is known, sits on her porch one afternoon in early June. She sees her neighbor, Matthew Cuthbert, leaving his home. This activity is surprising, since the painfully shy Matthew is known as a bit of a recluse. Even more surprising is that fact that he is wearing his best suit and driving his buggy, evidence that an important errand calls him away. Mrs. Rachel, her mind abuzz with questions, goes to the Cuthbert house to seek an explanation.

Matthew and Marilla Cuthbert live tucked away on a farm called Green Gables. Marilla, though more talkative than Matthew, is severe and private. Her house and her appearance reflect this severity: the immaculate house seems too sterile for comfort, and Marilla has an angular face and tightly knotted hair. Despite her stiffness, however, something about her mouth suggests a natural, if undeveloped, sense of humor.

When Mrs. Rachel asks about Matthew's errand, Marilla informs her that he is on his way to pick up the Cuthberts' new orphan from the train station. With Matthew getting older—he is sixty—they realized they needed help around the farm and decided to adopt a boy from the orphanage. This news shocks Mrs. Rachel, who launches into a monologue about the horror stories she has heard about orphans—a boy who set fire to his new home, another who used to suck eggs, and a girl who put strychnine in the well. Marilla acknowledges her concerns about bringing a stranger into the house, but she comforts herself with the knowledge that the boy will at least be Canadian and thus not too different from themselves. Marilla wonders why anyone would adopt a girl, since girls cannot work on farms.

Summary — Chapter 2:
Matthew Cuthbert Is Surprised

Matthew enjoys his quiet ride to the train station, except for the moments when he passes women and must nod at them. All women scare him, except for Marilla, who we learn is his sister, and Mrs. Rachel. He always feels like women are laughing at him. Arriving at the station, he sees no sign of the train and nobody on the platform except for a little girl and the stationmaster. Shyly avoiding the girl's eyes, he asks the stationmaster whether Mrs. Spencer has arrived with his orphan, and the stationmaster says that she has and that the delivery is waiting at the end of the platform.

A girl of about eleven years is sitting on a pile of shingles. She carries only a faded carpetbag as luggage and wears an ill-fitting, ugly dress and a faded hat, out of which snake two thick braids of red hair. Her face suggests spirit and vivacity: her big eyes change from green to gray depending on the light, and her mouth is large and expressive. Afraid of the social ordeal ahead, Matthew approaches the girl, who spares him from having to introduce himself. She confidently holds out her hand to him and starts talking. Words spill out of her mouth at a pace that shocks the quiet Matthew. She explains that while she waited, she imagined an alternate plan for the evening in case Matthew did not come for her. She would have climbed a nearby wild cherry tree and slept among the blooms and moonshine, imagining she was sleeping in marble halls. Although Matthew is surprised that a girl, rather than the boy he expected, sits before him, he decides to take her to Green Gables for the night and let Marilla tell the girl they will not be able to keep her.

Anne rarely pauses from her chatter during the ride to Green Gables. Through her monologue, she reveals a vivid imagination and a thirst for beauty, along with a tendency to criticize herself, especially her red hair. She repeatedly remarks on the beauty of the landscape and exclaims that calling Avonlea her home is a dream come true. She compares the lush trees of Avonlea to the scrawny saplings at the orphanage, and although she loves the new landscape, she expresses sympathy for the undernourished orphanage trees, with which she feels a sense of camaraderie. Arriving at the Cuthbert place, Anne gushes that Green Gables feels like home, a home more beautiful and perfect than any she could have imagined.

Summary—Chapter 3: Marilla Cuthbert Is Surprised

Unlike Matthew, Marilla does not shrink from voicing her surprise upon seeing a girl orphan, instead of a boy, at her front door. As the Cuthberts talk about Mrs. Spencer's mistake, Anne realizes she is not wanted. She dramatically bursts into tears, crying, "Nobody ever did want me. I might have known it was all too beautiful to last." Marilla and Matthew worriedly look at each other over the weeping child.

Marilla interrupts the girl's outpouring to ask her name. Anne replies that she would like to be called Cordelia because she thinks the name elegant. Pressed to reveal her real name, she admits that it is Anne. She considers her name plain and unromantic, but likes the fact that her name is spelled with an "e," which she feels makes it far more distinguished than if it were "Ann." Marilla dismisses Anne's musings about the spelling of her name with a quick "fiddlesticks." Anne, focused on her situation at the Cuthberts, cannot eat supper and mournfully explains that she is "in the depths of despair." She appeals to Marilla, asking if Marilla has ever been in the depths of despair. Marilla answers that she has not and cannot imagine what such a thing might feel like. After supper, Anne dons her skimpy orphanage nightgown and cries herself to sleep in the desolate spare room.

Downstairs, Marilla broaches the subject of how they will get rid of the unwanted girl. To her amazement, the usually passive Matthew voices an opinion, suggesting they might keep the child, who is so excited to stay at Green Gables and so sweet. When Marilla asks what good a girl would do on a farm, Matthew says, "We might be some good to her."

Summary—Chapter 4: Morning at Green Gables

Anne wakes up momentarily confused by her surroundings. Her confusion turns to delight and then to disappointment as she remembers that although she is at her new home, Matthew and Marilla do not want her. Her spirits improve at the sight of the morning sunshine and a beautiful cherry tree in full bloom outside her window. Marilla yanks her out of her daydream by ordering her to get dressed. The sharpness of Marilla's tone, we are told, belies a more gentle underlying nature, one that Anne seems to perceive and appreciate. Accustomed to an authoritarian upbringing, Anne is not cowed by Marilla's harshness or her admonishment that Anne talks too much.

At breakfast, Anne announces that she has regained her appetite and is happy because it is morning, and mornings provide "so much scope for imagination." Marilla hushes her, and Anne obediently quits her chattering. Throughout the silent meal Marilla feels increasingly uncomfortable, as though there is something unnatural in Anne's silence. After breakfast, Anne declares that she will not play outside, despite the beauty of the day, because it would make her love Green Gables too much, which would cause her even more pain upon leaving. Instead, she contents herself by communing with the houseplants, one of which she names Bonny.

Throughout the morning, Marilla vents inwardly; she can tell from Matthew's countenance that he still wants to keep Anne. She is frustrated by Matthew's silence, and wishes he would voice his opinion so that she could defeat him with a well-reasoned argument. In the afternoon, Marilla takes Anne in the buggy to visit Mrs. Spencer and sort out the mistake. As they are departing, Matthew says that he has just hired a boy to help on the farm, an arrangement that would allow them to keep Anne. Angry, Marilla does not reply.

Analysis—Chapters 1–4

Setting plays an important role in *Anne of Green Gables*. These chapters, in introducing the characters and their homes, suggest that houses reflect the personalities of their inhabitants. The Lyndes live on the main street, an appropriate place for them since Mrs. Rachel, the town snoop and gossip, likes to keep constant vigil over the activities of Avonlea. The Cuthberts live secluded on their farm, which reflects their reclusive natures. Marilla's meticulously clean kitchen and garden reflect her own severity. Montgomery suggests we should understand the characters that people this novel by examining their homes and surroundings.

Landscape not only establishes characters' identities; it also guides their interactions. Because Mrs. Rachel and Marilla live close to one another, they have become friends. They are not particularly compatible, but a comfortable coexistence has evolved between the two women. Mrs. Rachel's unannounced visit to Marilla seems to be one of her regular intrusions on Green Gables. The brook that runs from Green Gables to the Lynde place is a metaphor for the relationship between the two women. Its source at the Cuthbert place is silent, formed from a network of invisible trickles of water. By the time it reaches the Lynde plot, it has become a stream, a distinct and boisterous collection of all the quiet trickles of water from Green Gables. The stream also represents the way Mrs. Rachel collects bits and pieces of news and turns them into a steady flow of gossip.

Marilla seems to consider an orphan a pair of hands rather than a child with a personality and needs. She objects to Anne because she knows Anne could not work on the farm, not because she worries that she and Matthew are inexperienced with children. The difference between Anne's warmth and optimism and Marilla's sternness begins a dynamic that foreshadows how much Anne causes the Cuthberts to change their routine.

Matthew and Marilla live together much like a married couple. Montgomery portrays both sister and brother as nearly sexless beings; Matthew cannot even look women in the eye, and Marilla is straitlaced and stern. However, some view their cohabitation as slightly strange. Mrs. Rachel seems scandalized at the prospect of Matthew and Marilla raising a child, perhaps in part because raising a child together suggests a married relationship. In a biographical article about her career, Montgomery wrote that incest was common in the town where she grew up; however, she makes no implication that incest exists in Matthew and Marilla's relationship, suggesting instead that a brother and sister can live together and even, despite Mrs. Rachel's protestations, raise a child together in a natural way. She emphasizes this point by having Anne call her new guardians "Matthew" and "Marilla" rather than "Mother" and "Father," or even "Aunt" and "Uncle."

CHAPTERS 5–8

SUMMARY—CHAPTER 5: ANNE'S HISTORY
Anne announces that she is determined to enjoy the ride back to Mrs. Spencer's orphanage. Marilla, realizing that Anne must talk about something, decides to pick the topic herself, and asks Anne about her past. Anne says she would prefer to tell what she imagines about herself, as her imagination is so much richer than her history, but she agrees to tell her story. Her parents, Walter and Bertha Shirley, were teachers, and both died of fever when Anne was a baby. She was adopted by Mrs. Thomas, a poor woman with a drunken husband, who wanted Anne only so she would have help with her children. Eight years later, after the death of Mr.

Thomas, Mrs. Thomas gave Anne to another poor woman, Mrs. Hammond, and Anne cared for Mrs. Hammond's three sets of twins. After two years, Mr. Hammond died, and Anne was sent to the orphanage, where she lived for four months. She received little schooling but compensated for her lack of formal education by reading voraciously.

After hearing Anne's sad history, Marilla pities her for the first time. Anne, however, refuses to feel sorry for herself, crediting her various foster mothers with good intentions, even if the women were not always kind. Marilla begins to consider keeping Anne. She thinks Anne ladylike and supposes Anne could easily be trained out of her bad habits.

Summary — Chapter 6: Marilla Makes Up Her Mind
Marilla and Anne arrive at Mrs. Spencer's orphanage and explain the mistake. Mrs. Spencer apologizes and says that the situation will work out for the best anyway. Another woman, Mrs. Peter Blewett, wants to adopt a girl to help with her rambunctious children, so Anne can be handed over to her, allowing the Cuthberts to adopt the boy they originally wanted. This news does not please Marilla, for Mrs. Blewett is known for her nastiness and stinginess, and for driving her servants hard. Marilla feels a twinge of guilt at the thought of relinquishing Anne to her. Mrs. Blewett comes to borrow a recipe from Mrs. Spencer, and her presence terrifies Anne. Marilla takes Anne back to Green Gables, saying she needs time to think about the proposition.

At home, she tells Matthew that she is willing to keep Anne if he agrees not to interfere with her child-rearing methods. Marilla admits to nervousness at the prospect of raising a girl but tells Matthew, "Perhaps an old maid doesn't know much about bringing up a child, but I guess she knows more than an old bachelor." Matthew, delighted by Marilla's decision, asks only that Marilla be good and kind to Anne. Marilla reflects that she has invited a challenge into her life. She cannot quite believe what she is about to do, and she is even more surprised that Matthew, famous for his fear of women, is so adamant about keeping Anne. She decides to wait until the following day to tell Anne of their decision.

Summary — Chapter 7: Anne Says Her Prayers

At bedtime, Marilla begins her program of moral and social education for Anne. She scolds Anne for leaving her clothes all over the floor the previous night and for failing to pray before bed. Anne replies that she has never said a prayer and does not know how to pray, though she would be happy to learn. Anne begins to ruminate on the language of prayer and religion. At the asylum, she was taught that God is "infinite, eternal, and unchangeable," a description she thought grand. She explains that she rejected God because Mrs. Thomas told her God gave her red hair on purpose.

Despite her distaste for God, Anne wants to oblige Marilla. Marilla, horrified that a near-heathen is staying under her roof, begins to teach Anne the prayer "Now I lay me down to sleep," but she senses that this prayer for innocent children is inappropriate for Anne, who has already had such a hard life. She lets Anne create her own prayer, and Anne improvises a flowery speech thanking God for such gifts as Bonny the geranium and the White Way of Delight, which is what she calls the main road of Avonlea. She prays for Green Gables to become her home, and to become pretty when she grows up. She ends the prayer by saying, "Yours respectfully, Anne Shirley." Marilla resolves to send Anne to Sunday school as soon as she can make her some proper clothes.

Summary — Chapter 8: Anne's Bringing-Up Is Begun

The next afternoon, Anne begs Marilla to tell her whether she can stay at Green Gables. Marilla makes Anne wash the dishcloth in hot water before announcing that she can stay. When Anne hears the good news, she cries with happiness, promising to be good and obedient, two qualities she senses Marilla values above all others. Anne asks whether she should continue to refer to Marilla as Miss Cuthbert or whether she might call her Aunt Marilla. Calling Marilla her aunt, says Anne, would be almost as good as having an actual relative. Marilla says Anne should call her Marilla.

Afraid that Anne might repeat the prayer debacle of the previous night, Marilla instructs Anne to retrieve a copy of the Lord's Prayer from the next room and memorize it. Anne does not return for ten minutes. Marilla finds her kneeling before a picture entitled "Christ Blessing Little Children," rapt and starry-eyed. Anne is imagining herself as a little girl in the picture whom the other children ignore but who creeps into the crowd hoping for Christ's attention and blessing. Marilla chastises her for being irreverent, which surprises Anne.

Anne sits at the kitchen table to memorize Lord's Prayer. She asks Marilla if she will have a "bosom friend" or "kindred spirit" at Avonlea. Marilla says a little girl named Diana Barry lives nearby, and Anne asks about Diana's hair color, saying red hair in a bosom friend would be unendurable. She tells Marilla about her previous best friends, both imaginary. At Mrs. Thomas's, she created an imaginary best friend to whom she spoke in the glass door of a bookcase. When she moved to Mrs. Hammond's, she found a new best friend in the echo of her own voice in a nearby valley. Marilla, fed up with Anne's chatter, sends her to her room, where she daydreams. She tries to imagine that she is Lady Cordelia Fitzgerald, but finding this persona unconvincing, she appeases herself with her new real name: Anne of Green Gables.

Analysis — Chapters 5–8

In these chapters, we learn that Anne has had a difficult life. She realizes that her foster mothers did not care for her; they simply wanted a maid and a babysitter. Considering the pain of Anne's life, her refusal to criticize her foster mothers makes her seem strong and surprisingly optimistic. She also expresses satisfaction in her friends, although they were imaginary. Along with her strength and optimism, Anne possesses a mature ability to use herself as a resource and find happiness in her own company.

Anne is guided not by the rules of social decorum but by her imagination, as Marilla recognizes when she lets Anne make up her own prayer rather than recite "Now I Lay Me Down to Sleep." For Anne, the reality that society presents can be altered by imagining a different reality. She thinks her own name and life dull, so she renames herself Cordelia and imagines herself a fine lady. She does not have friends, so she makes friends of her reflection and voice. She sees the good in people and places, and then imagines them as even better than they are.

Anne practices her own form of spirituality, which she has developed independently and which consists of a belief that miracles and perfection exist in life. Demoralizing experiences have turned her away from Christian tenets and toward a spiritual life centered on love of the natural world. Marilla cannot understand Anne's form of spirituality because it diverges from traditional religion. When Marilla asks Anne to pray in a Christian way, Anne begins to forge a mixture of her own spirituality and Marilla's religion. Anne prays before bed as Marilla's religion dictates, but she makes up her own flowery, unorthodox prayer. She looks at Marilla's picture of Christ, but she uses her imagination to insert herself into the scene.

Although Marilla disapproves of Anne's infractions, she does sympathize with Anne and begins to temper her sternness with sympathy. Although she insists that Anne call her Marilla instead of using the more affectionate name Aunt Marilla, she exhibits compassion for Anne, pitying her plight at the hands of cruel foster mothers, and refusing to hand her over to the unpleasant Mrs. Blewett. She does not even criticize Anne for her unorthodox prayer; although she comes down hard on Anne's improper behavior, she understands that Anne acts oddly not because of perversity or rebelliousness, but because she has never been taught differently. She seems to know that Anne has a good heart and wants to do the right thing.

Chapters 9–12

Summary—Chapter 9: Mrs. Rachel Lynde Is Properly Horrified

Two weeks after Anne's adoption, Mrs. Rachel Lynde drops by to inspect Anne. Talking with Mrs. Rachel, Marilla admits she feels affection for Anne: "I must say I like her myself ... the house seems a different place already." Mrs. Rachel disapproves of an old maid like Marilla attempting to raise a child. When Anne comes in from outside, Mrs. Rachel sizes her up, saying, "She's terrible skinny and homely, Marilla . . . And hair as red as carrots!" Anne flies into a fury, stomps her feet, and screams that she hates Mrs. Rachel. After calling Mrs. Rachel fat, clumsy, and devoid of imagination, she runs upstairs.

Mrs. Rachel, indignant and offended, advises Marilla to whip Anne and declares she will not visit Green Gables if she is to be treated in such a way. Rather than apologize for Anne, Marilla finds herself chastising Mrs. Rachel for being so insensitive. She is not horrified to learn that Anne has a temper; instead, Marilla is sympathetic to Anne, recognizing that she has never been taught how to behave, and she wants to laugh at Mrs. Rachel's snobbery. When Marilla goes upstairs, she finds Anne sobbing on her bed but utterly defiant. Anne maintains she had a right to be furious at being called skinny and homely. She asks Marilla to imagine how it feels to be called such things. Marilla remembers an incident from her own childhood in which an older lady called her homely, a comment that stung for years. Despite her sympathy for Anne, Marilla thinks Anne must be punished for lashing out at a visitor. She decides not to whip Anne but to make her apologize to Mrs. Rachel. Anne refuses, saying she cannot apologize for something she does not regret.

Summary — Chapter 10: Anne's Apology

Anne remains in her room the entire next day, sulking and barely touching the food Marilla brings her. Matthew, concerned about Anne, waits for Marilla to leave the house and then creeps up to Anne's room. He has not been upstairs for four years. He sneaks in and whispers to Anne that she should apologize to Mrs. Rachel, since Marilla is not likely to change her mind about the punishment. Anne admits that she is not as furious as she was, but says apologizing would be too humiliating. However, to oblige Matthew, she promises to go to Mrs. Rachel's. Stunned by his success with Anne, Matthew hurries away so Marilla won't find him interfering with Anne's punishment.

Anne tells Marilla she is willing to apologize, and they walk to Mrs. Rachel's house. During the first half of the walk, Anne's gait and countenance suggest her shame, but midway through the walk, her step quickens and her eyes become dreamy. Upon arriving at Mrs. Rachel's, Anne resumes slumping and throws herself on her knees before the older woman, clasping her hands and begging for forgiveness, saying,

> I could never express all my sorrow, no, not if I used up a whole dictionary . . . I'm a dreadfully wicked and ungrateful girl, and I deserve to be punished and cast out by respectable people for ever.

Mrs. Rachel accepts the apology readily. In her way, Mrs. Rachel atones for her own thoughtlessness by telling Anne that her red hair might darken into auburn as she grows up. She tells Marilla that despite Anne's odd ways, she likes her.

Marilla feels uneasy about Anne's apology. She recognizes that Anne enjoyed her punishment, making her apology theatrical and flowery. Although Marilla feels the punishment has backfired, she would feel odd chastising Anne for apologizing too well. As they walk home, Anne slips her hand into Marilla's, saying how happy

ANNE OF GREEN GABLES 25

she is to be going to a place that feels like home. At the touch of the little girl's hand, Marilla feels a rush of motherly warmth that is both pleasurable and disarming. She tries to restore her usual emotional control and fends off this unfamiliar feeling of affection by moralizing to Anne about good behavior.

SUMMARY — CHAPTER 11:
ANNE'S IMPRESSIONS OF SUNDAY SCHOOL
Marilla shows Anne the three new dresses she has made for her, all of which are ugly and none of which has the puffed sleeves that Anne wants. To make up for the ugliness of the dresses, Anne imagines they are as beautiful and ornate as the dresses she has seen other girls wearing. The next day, Anne goes to church and Sunday school alone, wearing one of her new dresses. On the way, she picks a bunch of flowers and decorates her otherwise plain hat with them, an eccentric adornment that causes other Avonlea churchgoers to scoff.

After church, Anne reports to Marilla that the service did not impress her. She says that the minister's sermon, the prayer, and the Sunday school teacher's prim questions were all unimaginative. Anne was able to survive the boring morning only by looking out the window and daydreaming. Marilla scolds Anne for her inattention at church but inwardly agrees with her. Although she never articulates her own criticisms of the minister, Mr. Bentley, and the Sunday school teacher, Mr. Bell, she, like Anne, has always felt that the church service is boring and uninspiring.

SUMMARY — CHAPTER 12: A SOLEMN VOW AND PROMISE
Mrs. Rachel tells Marilla that Anne put flowers in her hat at church, making herself the laughingstock of the congregation. When Marilla reprimands Anne for doing something so inappropriate, Anne bursts into tears. She does not understand what she did wrong, since the flowers were beautiful and other girls had artificial flowers in their hats. Anne's mood quickly changes when she learns they are to visit the Barrys that afternoon. Anne has dreamed of becoming bosom friends with Diana Barry, and she now trembles with nervousness. Marilla warns her not to say anything startling or to use too many big words in front of Mrs. Barry, who has a reputation for strictness.

At the Barry's house, Anne and Diana go out to the garden to play and immediately strike up a friendship. Anne's first words to Diana are a heartfelt proposition of friendship. She creates an oath of eternal devotion for them to swear. On the walk back to Green Gables, Anne blissfully tells Marilla that she has found a kindred spirit in the plump, pretty, raven-haired Diana. When Matthew gives Anne chocolates he has bought for her, Anne asks to be allowed to share them with Diana. She says she will enjoy her chocolate even more if she can give half of it to her new friend. Marilla, pleased by Anne's generous spirit, tells Matthew she cannot imagine what life would be like without Anne.

Analysis—Chapters 9–12

In each succeeding chapter, Montgomery illustrates her characters in greater depth and detail. Each chapter contains a small story, and as the stories accumulate, we can trace the evolution of the characters and their relationships with one another. In Chapters 9 through 12, Anne blows up at Mrs. Rachel, apologizes, goes to church, and meets Diana Barry. Over the course of these events, Anne demonstrates her willingness to learn and to follow the rules of society. She begins by throwing a wild tantrum, but she ends by apologizing for her bad deeds. Matthew changes too: at the beginning of the novel, he dislikes interacting with women, even hesitating to nod at them on the street. In these chapters, however, he becomes a warm father figure who takes increasing pleasure in spoiling Anne. Matthew and Anne are "kindred spirits," and in his dealings with Anne, Matthew shows a flair for parenting. In Chapter 10, for instance, Anne agrees to apologize to Mrs. Rachel not because it is the right thing to do or because Marilla threatens her but because she wants to oblige Matthew.

Anne struggles to do the right thing, but Avonlea's code of manners is unfamiliar to her, and she acts like a well-meaning tourist in a foreign country, violating the standards of propriety by accident. Although anxious to do what people consider right, Anne acts according to her own moral code. She feels that because Mrs. Rachel insults her, she has a right to show her anger, and because she does not truly believe she should apologize to Mrs. Rachel, she makes the apology a piece of theater. Anne's moral code contrasts with Marilla's. Marilla frequently observes something Anne does, like decorating her hat with wildflowers, and deems it ridiculous because it is unconventional. Anne, however, does not understand how she can be considered bad when her behavior makes perfect sense to her and when she is not trying to hurt anyone.

ANNE OF GREEN GABLES

Despite her criticisms of Anne, Marilla changes over the course of these chapters, even revising her own moral code because of Anne's different perspective. Sometimes when Marilla feels she should reprimand Anne, she thinks about the logic of such a scolding and decides against criticizing. For example, when Anne returns from church and calls the preacher unimaginative and boring, Marilla admits to herself that she shares these exact feelings, although she has been unwilling to acknowledge them in the past. As Marilla and Anne begin to understand each other better, they start to question their own standards of judgment and to accept each other's moral codes.

Chapters 13–16

Summary—Chapter 13: The Delights of Anticipation

Marilla fumes as she looks out the window and sees Anne talking to Matthew forty-five minutes after she was supposed to go inside and do chores. Marilla's anger diminishes as Anne bursts into the room and joyfully describes the Sunday school picnic planned for the following week. She cannot wait to attend and to have her first taste of ice cream. When Marilla agrees to let her attend and says she will bake a basket of food for Anne to take along, Anne flies into her arms and kisses her cheek. Marilla flushes with warmth, though she disguises her pleasure with an injunction to Anne to be more obedient. Anne talks excitedly about her adventures with Diana and especially about their playhouse in the woods, which is composed of discarded pieces of board and china.

When Marilla tries to hush Anne and quell her excitement about the upcoming picnic, Anne replies that she would rather look forward to things and risk disappointment than follow advice from stodgy ladies like Mrs. Rachel who say, "Blessed are they who expect nothing for they shall not be disappointed." Anne says she was disappointed when she finally saw a diamond because it was not half as beautiful as she had imagined. She envisioned that a diamond was as colorful as the best amethyst, a stone that pleases both Anne and Marilla. Marilla has an amethyst brooch, her most prized possession, which she wears to church. Anne loves it so much that she begs Marilla to let her hold it for a minute.

SUMMARY & ANALYSIS

Summary—Chapter 14: Anne's Confession

Two days before the picnic, Marilla notices that her brooch is missing. She asks Anne if she touched it, and Anne admits that while Marilla was out for the afternoon, she saw it in Marilla's room and tried it on just for a moment. Marilla, after searching her room thoroughly, realizes that Anne must have lost the brooch. Anne denies she lost it, steadfastly maintaining that she put it back. Marilla, however, cannot reconcile Anne's story with the fact that the brooch is nowhere to be found, and she sends Anne to her room, declaring that she must stay there until she confesses.

On the day of the picnic, Anne decides to confess. In poetic, theatrical language, she explains that she borrowed the brooch so that she could imagine she was Lady Cordelia and then accidentally dropped it into the Lake of Shining Waters. Marilla is furious that Anne lied and that she seems to feel no remorse. She orders Anne to stay in her room and tells her she cannot attend the picnic—a sentence Anne thinks unjust, since Marilla promised she could leave her room once she confessed. Anne throws a fit. Matthew suggests that Marilla is being a bit harsh, but he cannot think of a good defense for Anne.

Marilla, trying to busy herself with chores, goes to fetch a black shawl that needs mending. When she picks it up, she catches sight of the brooch hanging from a thread. Realizing she was at fault the whole time and that Anne was telling the truth when she said she didn't lose it, Marilla goes to Anne to apologize. She feels sorry for treating Anne as she did and has to squelch a desire to laugh at Anne's invented confession. She scolds Anne for confessing to a deed she did not commit but admits she forced Anne to lie. Anne goes to her picnic and comes home overjoyed, telling stories about her adventures and about the indescribable taste of ice cream.

Summary—Chapter 15: A Tempest in the School Teapot

Anne and Diana take the most scenic route to school every day, walking on roads Anne has renamed Lover's Lane and Willowmere and Violet Vale. Anne is thrilled to have a bosom friend in Diana and is willing to overlook Diana's average imagination. Because Anne loves Diana so much, she lets Diana call a place the Birch Path, even though the name lacks Anne's spark of originality. Marilla had worried that Anne's temper, talkativeness, and oddities would cause her trouble at school, but Anne turns out to be a smart pupil and quickly

ANNE OF GREEN GABLES 29

adjusts. The other girls include her in their potluck lunches and exchange of small gifts. Anne dislikes boys and does not like the idea of flirting with them, though she is humiliated by the thought that boys are unlikely to flirt with her.

Anne's world expands from the quiet life at Green Gables to the bustling gossipy schoolroom at Avonlea. Her usual chatter to Marilla about flowers and nature changes to reports on school. The teacher, Mr. Phillips, pays little attention to the pupils in his one-room school and lets them run amok as he sits in the back row flirting with the oldest student, Prissy Andrews. Prissy is sixteen and studying for her entrance exam to college.

Though Anne has received little schooling previously and is consequently one reading level behind her peers, she is quickly recognized as the smartest in the class. She takes pride in her intelligence, although she says she would rather be beautiful than smart. As Diana and Anne walk to school one day, Diana warns Anne she should not take for granted her status as smartest pupil, since Gilbert Blythe, the handsomest and smartest boy at school, will soon return to class. When she sees Gilbert, Anne agrees that he is handsome. But, unlike all the other girls, she is uninterested in him. Intrigued by the new girl who refuses to look at him, Gilbert tries to get her attention. He reaches across the aisle and whispers "Carrots," as he tweaks her braid. Anne's quick temper flares, and she jumps up, yelling at him and smashing a slate over his head.

Mr. Phillips, busy flirting with Prissy, ignores Gilbert's attempt to take the blame, refuses to listen to Anne's side of the story, and punishes her by making her stand in front of the class for the rest of the day. Several times, Gilbert tries to apologize and make peace with Anne, but she ignores him each time. The next day, Mr. Phillips decides to make an example of pupils who return to school late after the lunch break. The boys and Anne, who is daydreaming alone, arrive late. Rather than go through the trouble of punishing all the latecomers, Mr. Phillips picks Anne out of the crowd and makes her sit next to Gilbert Blythe, a punishment Anne thinks unfair and humiliating. At the end of the day, Anne packs up her desk and solemnly tells Diana that sitting next to Gilbert was excruciating and that she will never return to school.

Anne goes home and tells Marilla she will not go back to school. Marilla sympathizes with Anne. She goes to Mrs. Rachel for advice and decides that she will let Anne stay at home until she wants to return to school.

Summary—Chapter 16:
Diana Is Invited to Tea with Tragic Results

One beautiful October morning, Marilla announces that she will be away for the day and says that Anne should assume responsibility for running the house. She adds that Anne may invite Diana over for tea, leaving specific instructions about what Anne can serve Diana. During their tea, the girls, clad in their second-best dresses, act ladylike and proper, inquiring after each other's health and families until Anne suggests they go outside and pick apples, at which point they resume their normal girlish familiarity.

When the girls return inside for tea, Diana accepts a cup of raspberry cordial, a drink reserved for special occasions that Marilla has given the girls permission to drink that day. As Diana drinks a second glass and then a third, Anne tells stories about her ineptness in the kitchen. One time, she forgot to put flour in a cake. Another time, she neglected to cover plum-pudding sauce with a cloth, which she was using as a white veil. The next day, she found a mouse drowned in the sauce; she had planned to tell Marilla, but then got lost in another daydream. Two very stylish people came to tea, and just as Marilla was about to serve the plum pudding and sauce, Anne remembered her mistake and shouted out the whole mouse story, much to Marilla's embarrassment. When Anne finishes her story, Diana stands up unsteadily and announces she does not feel well and must leave. Anne presses her to stay, but Diana insists on stumbling home.

Two days later, Anne hears from Mrs. Rachel that Diana was not sick but drunk. Marilla realizes that Anne mistook the bottle of red currant wine for raspberry cordial and accidentally gave Diana alcohol. Mrs. Barry is furious, assuming that Anne intentionally intoxicated Diana. When Marilla goes to explain to Mrs. Barry that Anne made an innocent mistake, she is met with a stony countenance and harsh words. Mrs. Barry will not forgive Anne and has ordered Diana never to speak to Anne again. Anne begs Mrs. Barry to soften her sentence, but Mrs. Barry is resolute. Anne despairs at the prospect of being separated from Diana forever.

Analysis—Chapters 13–16

The schoolroom at Avonlea absorbs Anne and becomes the focus of her world. For the first time, Anne befriends many children her age. Instead of talking to plants or her reflection, as she did in the orphan asylum, she find people with whom she can interact. Although she has not had any practice socializing with peers, she manages to learn quickly the rules and manners of the social world. Similarly, her lack of formal education does not prevent her from absorbing the rules of reading, writing, and mathematics. As Anne tries to make sense of the new rules, she has some difficulty reconciling them with her own code of behavior. For example, Diana and all the other girls are accustomed to Gilbert Blythe's barbs and have grown to enjoy attention from him. Anne, a stranger to such friendly teasing, is offended and enraged when he calls her "Carrots." Unfamiliar with the ways in which young people interact with each other, she cannot understand that Gilbert's comment is not meant to be an insult but is rather just an instance of teasing.

As Anne's social world changes, the content of her communication changes. Before, she talks to Marilla about nature and her imagination, but now she cannot stop talking about school events and friends. Her absorption in the minutiae of the girls' social events reveals that, despite her eccentricities, Anne is not fundamentally different from the other girls her age. Her quick assimilation into the society of the schoolhouse suggests the power of peers to influence behavior, as well as the human ability to learn rapidly and conform to cultural norms.

The schoolroom replicates the adult world. The girls gossip as Mrs. Rachel does, for example, and their play mimics adult behavior. At tea, Anne and Diana act ladylike in imitation of their elders. Montgomery illustrates the danger of mimicking adult behavior with the episode of Diana's drunkenness. Although Marilla and Mrs. Barry constantly prepare their girls to act like proper adults, when the girls make an innocent mistake in the process of trying to act grown up, the adults punish them.

Marilla continues to change and become a better parent. Just as Anne has to apologize earlier for lashing out at Mrs. Rachel, in these chapters Marilla learns to apologize for her mistaken assumptions. She feels bad about forcing Anne to lie and admits to her own mistake. Marilla becomes increasingly effective at managing Anne's stubbornness and hot temper. When Anne comes home from school set on never returning, Marilla agrees to let her stay home. This leniency is new to Marilla, a product of her growing understanding of Anne and the mellowing effect that Anne has on her.

Chapters 17–20

Summary—Chapter 17: A New Interest in Life

One afternoon, Anne spies Diana outside beckoning to her. Anne rushes out, and Diana tells her she is still forbidden to play with Anne so she has come to say goodbye. The two have a sentimental, melodramatic parting. When Diana cries that she loves her bosom friend, Anne says, "Nobody ever has loved me since I can remember. Oh, this is . . . a ray of light which will forever shine on the darkness of a path severed from thee, Diana." Anne asks for a lock of Diana's black hair to keep as a memento. To combat her despair over losing Diana, Anne decides to return to school. There, she can look at Diana even though the two are forbidden to talk or play together. Anne's classmates welcome her back with open arms and little gifts. Some of the girls send her plums, bottles, or copied poems, and two admiring boys, Charlie Sloane and Gilbert Blythe, pass her a slate pencil and an apple, respectively. Anne graciously accepts Charlie's gift but ostentatiously ignores Gilbert's offering. One day, to Anne's dismay, she and Gilbert are tied as top student, and Mr. Phillips writes both of their names on the board.

Summary—Chapter 18: Anne to the Rescue

A Canadian premier comes to Prince Edward Island to address a mass meeting in Charlottetown, about thirty miles from Avonlea. Mrs. Rachel loves political events, so she goes with her husband and Marilla. At home, Anne is studying, and Matthew is reading the Farmers' Advocate when Diana rushes into the house and cries that her three-year-old sister Minnie May is sick with the croup, and neither she nor the babysitter know what to do. Matthew quickly harnesses the horse and goes for the doctor, while Anne and Diana rush back to the Barry house, Orchard Slope. Having cared for three sets of twins at Mrs. Hammond's home who all got croup regularly, Anne knows how to care for Minnie May. Matthew arrives with the doctor at three A.M., by which time Minnie May is sleeping peacefully.

Later, the doctor tells Mr. and Mrs. Barry that Anne saved their daughter's life. Mrs. Barry comes to Green Gables the following day and apologizes for blaming Anne for the currant wine incident. She invites Anne to tea and encourages her to be friends with Diana once again. Anne is thrilled by the news and pleased that the Barrys treat her like special company at tea.

SUMMARY — CHAPTER 19:
A CONCERT, A CATASTROPHE, AND A CONFESSION
Anne explains to Marilla that in celebration of Diana's birthday, Mrs. Barry has agreed to let Diana invite Anne to a Debating Club concert and spend the night in the Barrys' spare bedroom. Anne can hardly contain her excitement, but Marilla declares that she cannot go because little girls have no business at late-night concerts. Matthew disagrees with Marilla's decision and tells her so until she relents and gives Anne permission to go. On the day of the concert, Anne and Diana take pleasure in everything from getting dressed to riding Diana's cousins' pung sleigh to listening to scholars recite poetry and sing at the concert. After the concert, they return to the Barrys' house. They change into their nightgowns, and Anne proposes that they race to the spare bedroom. The girls charge in and leap onto the bed, landing right on Diana's crotchety aunt, Miss Josephine Barry, who arrived for her visit unexpectedly early.

Anne is disappointed at having to sleep with the toddler, Minnie May, rather than in the spare bedroom, but the following day returns to Green Gables happy and satisfied. Later, Mrs. Rachel reports that the Barry house has been in an uproar all afternoon. Aunt Josephine, angered at being awoken in the middle of the night, has decided to cut short her visit and rescind her offer to pay for Diana's music lessons. She is a rich old lady, used to being treated decorously, and will not listen to Diana's pleas. Anne wants to remedy the situation since she, not Diana, proposed the race into the spare bedroom. She goes to the Barry house and enters the old lady's room, terrified but bold, and begins to confess. The old lady is amused by Anne's elevated way of speaking. She agrees to give Diana her music lessons and stay the full month at Avonlea, under the condition that Anne talk to her at the Barrys' and then visit her in town.

SUMMARY — CHAPTER 20:
A GOOD IMAGINATION GONE WRONG
Spring returns to Green Gables, bringing Anne's favorite ornaments of nature—flowers. She tells Marilla stories about exploring nature with her school friends. On the day of her anniversary of arriving at Green Gables, Anne takes considerable care with her chores. Marilla leaves Anne in charge of the house because of a headache. In the evening, Marilla asks Anne to go to Mrs. Barry to get an apron pattern. Anne asks Marilla if she may delay the trip

until morning. She explains that she and Diana, tired of their commonplace surroundings, have begun to pretend that the woods between their houses are haunted. But Marilla, always trying to rid Anne of the nonsense in her head, sends her on the errand. Anne returns from the Barrys' house out of breath from running and trembling with fear.

Analysis — Chapters 17–20

The anniversary of Anne's arrival at Green Gables corresponds with signs of Anne's development as a young woman and a full member of Avonlea society. Anne digests her old experiences and uses them to improve herself, a process central to a child's development into adolescence and adulthood. In an instance of Anne's increasing maturity, she manages for the first time to make a heartfelt, effective apology. In contrast to her overblown apologies to Mrs. Rachel and Marilla in past chapters, Anne's apology to Aunt Josephine, in Chapter 19, is delicate, sincere, and immediately successful. She has learned to curb her temper and put her eloquence to good use.

Anne applies old lessons to new situations not only when making apologies but also when saving Minnie May. Although Anne disliked caring for Mrs. Hammond's twins, she is able to use the knowledge she gained in the Hammond household to save Minnie May's life. Previously, Anne's unorthodox background and unusual behavior have made her the town laughingstock, but in these chapters respectable people like the doctor compliment her for learning from the unusual experiences of her past.

Anne and Gilbert's rivalry grows increasingly heated. Anne is "as intense in her hatreds as in her loves," an intensity apparent in her enduring hatred for Gilbert. She will not even speak Gilbert's name, as if trying to deny his existence altogether. When Mr. Phillips writes their names on the board in Chapter 17, the image of Anne's name underneath that of her enemy suggests both a flirtation between the two of them and her failure to best him in school, and Anne cringes at the sight. However, just as Anne's unorthodox manner of speaking wins her the approval of Aunt Josephine, her unusual talent for holding a grudge works in her favor in some respects. Because she loathes Gilbert and wants to triumph over him, she works harder in school than she otherwise might, even given her natural love of learning.

Anne displays her fanciful and unshakable imagination yet again in pretending with Diana that the woods between their houses are haunted. There is nothing scary about these woods, but Anne simply decides that she wants them to evoke a particular emotional reaction. Because she believes so strongly in this fantasy, she actually alters her perception of reality. Though she herself has created the idea that the woods are scary, she nevertheless comes home nervous with fright. This ability to get lost in fantasy and think creatively about the world differentiates Anne from Marilla, who initially cannot even fathom that Anne could be useful at Green Gables.

Chapters 21–24

Summary—Chapter 21:
A New Departure in Flavorings

On the last day of June, Anne returns from school with red eyes and a soaked handkerchief in her hand. The universally disliked schoolteacher, Mr. Phillips, is leaving his job, and his farewell speech made all the girls cry. The old minister, Mr. Bentley, has also given up his post, and the Avonlea congregation chooses a young man named Mr. Allan as Mr. Bentley's successor. The congregation welcomes Mr. Allan and his pretty young wife into the community. Anne admires Mrs. Allan, who teaches Anne's Sunday school class, because unlike the previous teacher she encourages the students to ask many questions.

Marilla invites Mr. and Mrs. Allan to tea, and works for days preparing a generous spread of food for the young couple. Marilla allows Anne to bake a layer cake. Even though Anne has baked many cakes, she is nervous nonetheless. The cake comes out of the oven looking beautiful, and Anne is proud to serve it to her new hero, Mrs. Allan. Mrs. Allan can hardly swallow the cake, but she eats it to spare Anne's feelings. When Marilla tastes the cake herself, she asks Anne what ingredients she used. Marilla discovers that Anne accidentally used anodyne liniment instead of vanilla, making the cake taste awful. Anne is mortified and runs upstairs, throws herself on the bed, and weeps. Mrs. Allan cheers Anne up, and Anne begins to see some good in the embarrassing situation, saying at least she never makes the same mistake twice. She is relieved to think that once she has made all possible mistakes, she will be done making mistakes for good.

Summary — Chapter 22: Anne Is Invited Out to Tea

Returning from the post office, Anne is filled with excitement because Mrs. Allan has invited her to tea. Marilla explains that Mrs. Allan has invited all the children in her Sunday school class, but this news does not diminish Anne's excitement. As usual, Marilla is troubled by Anne's enthusiasm, believing it will cause Anne pain when reality does not live up to her expectations. Anne is nervous that she will forget her manners and offend Mrs. Allan. Marilla gives her etiquette advice and tells her not to think about how she should behave but to imagine what sorts of behavior would please Mrs. Allan. After tea, Anne describes her time at Mrs. Allan's home. She admires Mrs. Allan so much that she says she wants to become a minister's wife. She tells Marilla that, according to Mrs. Rachel, the school is getting a new teacher named Miss Muriel Stacy.

Summary — Chapter 23:
Anne Comes to Grief in an Affair of Honor

At the end of summer, Diana Barry invites all the girls in the Sunday school class to her house for a party. Tired of their usual songs and games, the girls decide to embark on more adventurous activities. They dare each other to hop around the yard on one foot or climb a tree. Josie Pye, a sly girl whom Diana and Anne dislike, dares Anne to walk the ridgepole of the Barry's kitchen roof. Diana tries to dissuade Anne from performing such a difficult dare, but Anne feels her honor is at stake, so she climbs to the top of the roof. She manages to walk a few steps before losing her balance, falling to the ground, and breaking her ankle. All the girls rush to her side, shrieking and crying.

When Marilla sees Mr. Barry carrying Anne back to Green Gables, she is terrified that something serious has happened. She realizes for the first time how much Anne means to her. Anne rests in bed for seven weeks and is pleased to find that many people in Avonlea care enough about her to visit. From her friends she hears all about the new teacher, Miss Stacy, who dresses beautifully and organizes recitations, nature walks, and physical exercises for her class. Anne thinks her new teacher will be a kindred spirit.

Summary — Chapter 24:
Miss Stacy and Her Pupils Get Up a Concert

Anne enjoys her return to school in October. She especially adores her new teacher, and flourishes academically and personally in Miss

Stacy's innovative schoolhouse. Both Mrs. Rachel and Marilla disapprove of Miss Stacy's novel teaching methods, which include sending boys to retrieve birds' nests from the tops of trees to use as teaching tools and leading the children in daily exercises. In November, Miss Stacy announces that the school will put on a Christmas concert to raise money to buy a Canadian flag for the schoolhouse. Anne is even more excited than the rest of the students and anxiously awaits the performance of her two recitations. Marilla declares the concert "foolishness," so Anne talks to Matthew about the concert. He reflects that he is glad that he has no part in bringing up Anne, since his lack of involvement allows him to spoil her.

Analysis — Chapters 21–24

Anne benefits from the teaching methods of Mrs. Allan and Miss Stacy. Education under Mr. Phillips, Marilla, and Mr. Bell, Anne's former Sunday school teacher, consists of memorizing and reciting facts and moral lessons, which grates on Anne's imaginative spirit. The more interesting, innovative methods of Mrs. Allan and Miss Stacy fit better with Anne's learning style. In addition to learning schoolwork more readily, Anne begins to learn the nature of adulthood from her new teachers. When Mrs. Allan comforts her after the cake mishap, Anne begins to think more forgivingly of her own mistakes, telling Marilla that at least she learns from her errors.

Anne's views about religion and school change because of her friendships with Mrs. Allan and Miss Stacy. Previously, Anne says her prayers to oblige Marilla, but the pretty and kind Mrs. Allen helps Anne see that organized religion need not be painful or boring. For Anne, religion no longer means foreign, dull speeches and rules; under Mrs. Allan's tutelage, religion becomes interesting, especially because Mrs. Allan allows her pupils to ask questions about it. Similarly, Miss Stacy's new, liberal form of education allows Anne to enjoy learning for its own sake. When Anne first comes to Avonlea, she advances quickly in her studies in order to irk her rival, Gilbert, but this model of academic success depends largely on the presence of an enemy. Now, Anne can rely on herself alone. She sees that learning can be an exercise of imagination rather than a chore of rote memorization.

Marilla's affection for Anne continues to grow. When she sees Mr. Barry carrying Anne across the field, she realizes in a flash that she loves Anne more than she loves anything else in the world. Even what seems like unnecessary sternness is simply Marilla's affection for Anne. For example, when Marilla tries to dampen Anne's enthusiasm for the tea party, she does it not out of mean-spiritedness, but because she hates to think of Anne's hopes dashed, and wants to save her from disappointment.

Avonlea is a community caught between tradition and modernity, especially in its views on women. Characters such as Mrs. Rachel hold beliefs that seem to be in tension with one another. On the one hand, Mrs. Rachel feels that women should be given the right to vote—a liberal and progressive view. The Cuthberts, true to their generally conservative characters, oppose Mrs. Rachel in this belief. At the same time, however, Mrs. Rachel believes it "a dangerous innovation" for the Avonlea trustees to hire a female teacher. As women's roles change, Mrs. Rachel's contradictory views on women represent the Avonlea community as a whole. She does not wholly support independence and power for women, but she supports it in part. She believes simultaneously in tradition and in progress.

Chapters 25–28

Summary—Chapter 25:
Matthew Insists on Puffed Sleeves

On a cold December evening, Matthew enters the kitchen and realizes too late that Anne and her friends are already there conducting a rehearsal of "The Fairy Queen" in preparation for the Christmas concert. Shy of all the little girls, he stays silently in the corner until they leave. While observing the group, Matthew notices that Anne is dressed differently from her friends. He becomes convinced that she needs more fashionable clothing and goes into the town of Carmody to find a bright dress with puffed sleeves. Shopping is not an easy task for such a shy man, but Matthew summons his courage and goes to Samuel Lawson's store, which he thinks will not have a female clerk at the desk. Much to Matthew's dismay, he finds that Samuel Lawson has hired a female clerk, Miss Lucilla Harris.

Matthew is too scared to ask Miss Harris for fashion advice, and asks for twenty pounds of brown sugar and a garden rake before making his escape. Matthew eventually asks Mrs. Rachel for help, and she picks out a rich brown fabric and uses a fashionable pattern to make Anne's dress. Mrs. Rachel has often wondered why Marilla dresses Anne so plainly and is happy to have a part in updating Anne's wardrobe. On Christmas Day, Matthew unveils the dress, complete with puffed sleeves. Diana comes over with a present from Aunt Josephine for Anne: delicate slippers. Anne is delighted by her beautiful new garments.

Anne's Christmas concert is the first one Matthew and Marilla have been to in twenty years. Anne, wearing her new dress and shoes, is the star of the show. Both Cuthberts are swollen with pride. Matthew immediately tells Anne how proud he is of her, but Marilla decides not to compliment Anne.

SUMMARY — CHAPTER 26: THE STORY CLUB IS FORMED
After the excitement of the Christmas concert, the Avonlea students return to their normal, humdrum patterns. Anne, now almost thirteen, vows to improve herself by imitating Mrs. Allan, refraining from saying uncharitable things and trying to do good.

For school, the students are assigned to write a piece of fiction and a composition about a walk in the winter. These assignments displease Marilla because they rely on imagination rather than memorization. They elate Anne, however, and she completes her original story early. Diana moans that she does not have enough imagination to do the assignment. To help Diana cultivate her imagination and to practice her own writing, Anne proposes that the two girls start a story club. Two of their friends, Jane Andrews and Ruby Gillis, eventually join, and the girls spend their time inventing romantic, melodramatic storylines.

SUMMARY — CHAPTER 27:
VANITY AND VEXATION OF SPIRIT
One evening in late April, Marilla walks home feeling uplifted and lighthearted, though she does not realize that the sights of spring are the cause of her joy. She happily anticipates the warm fire and tea that Anne should have prepared for her at home. When she reaches Green Gables, Marilla finds the table bare and Anne nowhere to be found. She complains to Matthew that Anne has disobeyed her order to stay at home and prepare the meal. Her anger turns to concern when suppertime comes and there is still no sign of Anne. Marilla goes upstairs to get a candle from Anne's room and finds her lying facedown on her bed, moaning that she is too ugly to be seen. It turns out that Anne has dyed her hair with disastrous results. She bought hair dye from a traveling peddler who claimed the dye

would turn her hair raven black. The dye turned her hair green, and the only solution is for Marilla to crop it to an unfashionably short length. At first Anne weeps at the sight of herself in the mirror, but she then decides to look at her unattractive reflection to remind herself of the folly of vanity.

SUMMARY — CHAPTER 28: AN UNFORTUNATE LILY MAID
Anne, Diana, Ruby, and Jane enact a scene from a poem by Alfred Lord Tennyson in which the corpse of a character named Elaine is sent down a river in a barge. Though Anne does not look like Elaine, who has golden hair, she gets the part because none of the other girls want to drift down the pond alone in Mr. Barry's little boat. The girls recite romantic farewells and send Anne's unmoving body down the pond. For a few minutes, Anne revels in the romance of the situation, but she then feels water at her back. The boat has a leak, but Anne remains calm and prays for God to bring the boat close to one of the bridge piles (poles running vertically from the bridge to the bottom of the river) so she can grab on and wait for help. The girls see the boat sink, and, thinking that Anne has sunk with it, they run screaming for help. Anne is able to get to a bridge pile, however, where she hangs on and waits uncomfortably for help.

Just when Anne begins to think she cannot hold on any longer, Gilbert Blythe rows up and rescues her. After depositing her safely on the bank, he makes a friendly overture, apologizing again for calling her "Carrots" when they first met and complimenting the auburn color her hair has become. For a moment, Anne hesitates and considers befriending her sworn enemy. But she then recalls her humiliation during the "Carrots" incident and declares she will never become friends with him. Gilbert storms off. Meanwhile, Diana and Jane cannot find any adults to help and have become frantic. Ruby, always inclined toward hysteria, grieves at the Barry house. When Diana and Jane return to the pond, they are relieved that Anne is safe and thrilled by the romance of her rescue by Gilbert. Anne, however, orders Jane never to say the word "romantic" again.

ANALYSIS — CHAPTERS 25–28
To some extent, Matthew and Marilla reverse the characteristics traditionally associated with men and women. Matthew goes to great trouble to get Anne a new, fashionable dress, exhibiting almost

womanly qualities. Whereas Marilla thinks fashion silly, Matthew understands that Anne's dowdy dresses probably embarrass her; he sees the importance of fitting into one's peer group. Whereas Marilla is reserved and does not believe in spoiling children, exhibiting almost manly qualities, Matthew easily expresses his affection for Anne and welcomes every opportunity to dote on her.

Anne's approach to writing, which she describes in Chapter 26, reflects Montgomery's own approach. Anne writes romantic stories about ladies named Cordelia and Geraldine who fall in love and meet tragic ends. She explains to Marilla that the stories all have morals: the good people are rewarded and the bad people are punished. Similarly, Montgomery makes moral judgments about Anne's behavior. Montgomery does not divide the world into good and bad people, but she does reward Anne's strengths and punish her faults. Anne's mistakes never result in tragedy, but she meets with difficulties that are tragic in her perspective.

At the end of Chapter 28, Anne reflects on all of her mistakes. She realizes that each mistake has taught her an important lesson and that, taken together, the mistakes and lessons have made her a better person. After taking Marilla's brooch, for example, she learns not to play with things that don't belong to her. After running panicked through the woods, she learns to keep her imagination in check. After making cake with liniment, she learns to take care while cooking. After dyeing her hair, she learns to curb her vanity. Anne's faults and quirky traits, which Marilla and Mrs. Rachel enumerate at the beginning of Anne's stay, disappear with every mistake, chapter by chapter.

Although Anne's desire to rid herself of faults shows her maturation, she has not yet perfected herself. For example, she resolves to be modest after her vanity results in green hair, but her vanity over her hair makes her simmer afresh over a years-old insult and causes her to reject Gilbert's offer of friendship. Gilbert's rescue teaches Anne yet another lesson that demonstrates that she still has room to mature: real-life romance does not yet suit her. Although the boat episode has all the markings of the kind of fictional romance Anne loves—danger, a woman in distress, a last-minute rescue by a handsome man—Anne finds the event awkward, embarrassing, and irritating rather than charming and romantic.

Chapters 29–32

Summary—Chapter 29: An Epoch in Anne's Life

On a beautiful September evening, Anne is bringing the cows back from the pasture when she runs into Diana, who has exciting news: Aunt Josephine has invited the two girls to her mansion in Charlottetown to see an exhibition, an event similar to a fair. The girls go to Aunt Josephine's estate, called Beechwood, and they relish their drive. The house is richly decorated, with silk curtains, velvet carpets, and a spare bedroom specially made up for them. Anne finds that these luxuries, which she has dreamed about and yearned for, are actually disappointing and alienating in real life. She reflects later to Marilla that part of growing up is realizing that "[t]he things you wanted so much when you were a child don't seem half so wonderful to you when you get them."

The exhibition is exciting, with its displays of knitted lace, flowers, vegetables, and horseracing. Afterward, when Anne laments that she will have difficulty returning to normal life, Aunt Josephine offers to take the girls to a fancy restaurant for ice cream at eleven P.M. This restaurant visit comes to represent the excitement of city life to Anne. Upon returning home, Anne decides she would rather be sleeping in bed at Green Gables than gallivanting around a city.

Summary—Chapter 30: The Queen's Class Is Organized

One night Marilla rests after another one of her eye aches, which occur with increasing frequency and severity. She looks at Anne with an expression of fondness that she would never permit herself to show in the daylight when she could be seen. Because of Marilla's tendency to veil her affection, Anne does not know, we are told, that Marilla loves her so much. Marilla tells Anne that Miss Stacy visited that afternoon, and Anne, assuming Miss Stacy told Marilla about her recent misbehavior, quickly admits to sneaking a novel into class when she should have been studying. Anne also tells Marilla that she and Diana have been talking about serious subjects like the future and that they are thinking of becoming old maids and living together. Anne explains that Miss Stacy told the girls they must cultivate sound characters now, because once they reach their twenties the foundations of their characters will be set for life.

Marilla tells Anne that Miss Stacy has invited Anne to join a group of advanced scholars who will study every day after school to prepare for the entrance exam to Queen's Academy in a year and a half. Marilla says that every woman should be able to support herself and that teaching is a good profession for a woman. Anne hesitates to accept the offer to attend college because she worries that the cost of college will be too high for the Cuthberts. However, after Marilla says that Anne's education is worth the cost, Anne expresses excitement.

The other students in the advanced class are Gilbert Blythe, Ruby Gillis, Jane Andrews, Josie Pye, Charlie Sloane, and Moody Spurgeon MacPherson. They study for an hour every day, but begin to lose their drive when spring comes and the other students leave school early every day. For the first time since Minnie May was sick, Anne and Diana are separated, since the Barrys do not intend to send Diana to college.

The rivalry between Gilbert and Anne rekindles. Gilbert decides to treat Anne just as coldly as she treats him. This icy treatment distresses Anne, but she acts unconcerned. She realizes that she no longer feels angry with Gilbert, and she regrets causing tension.

The school year ends and Anne locks her books away, declaring that she wants to make the most of her last summer as a child. The next day Mrs. Rachel drops by Green Gables, and Marilla tells her that Matthew has had another bad spell with his heart, which is the first we hear of his condition. Marilla expresses her happiness that Anne is growing into a trustworthy person. Mrs. Rachel agrees that she was mistaken to doubt Anne when she arrived three years ago. She comments that Anne has improved in everything, especially in her looks. Though Anne lacks Diana's coloring and Ruby's flashy looks, there is something special and arresting in her "pale, big-eyed style."

Summary—Chapter 31:
Where the Brook and River Meet
After a rich summer free of studying, Anne returns to school with vigor and ambition. She is now fifteen years old, and with the other Avonlea scholars attends Debating Club concerts, parties, sleigh drives, and skating events. Anne is now taller than Marilla, and her eyes have grown serious. Anne does not chatter as she used to, explaining to Marilla that "it's nicer to think dear, pretty thoughts and keep them in one's heart." This change in Anne saddens

Marilla, who misses the bright-eyed child she first took in. She bursts into tears at the thought that next year Anne will go to college and leave Green Gables as quiet as it was before her arrival. Miss Stacy remains a central figure in Anne's education, especially in her training as a writer. Anne becomes critical of her own writing, changing her style from romantic to realistic. All the scholars are nervous about the upcoming entrance exam to Queen's Academy, and Anne has nightmares about failing.

Summary — Chapter 32: The Pass List Is Out

The end of June marks the end of Miss Stacy's tenure and Anne's time at Avonlea School. Anne and Diana walk home, weeping that their time together as child scholars has ended. Though Anne is paralyzed by nervousness about her upcoming entrance exam, she dutifully follows Miss Stacy's advice and avoids cramming during the week of the exam. After the first day of the exam, she writes Diana a letter from Charlottetown, relating the students' nervousness and comparing her own sense of foreboding to her fear when she first asked Marilla if she could stay at Green Gables.

Anne returns to Avonlea and greets Diana as though they had been apart for years. She spends an agonizing three weeks waiting for the results of the exam. Although Anne feels she has passed, she claims she would rather not pass at all than be beaten by her rival, Gilbert. Finally, the newspaper comes out with the results: Anne and Gilbert have tied for first place in the entire island, and all the Avonlea scholars have passed. Matthew, Marilla, Mrs. Rachel, and Diana are enormously proud of Anne's success.

Analysis — Chapters 29–32

Having used early chapters of the novel to establish Anne's character, in this section Montgomery shows the results of Anne's development and maturity. Anne is contented, lovely, and successful. After visiting Aunt Josephine, Anne realizes that the luxurious belongings for which she has always yearned do not satisfy her as she dreamed they would. She discovers that the ways of Avonlea suit her better than elegant city life. Even the critical Mrs. Rachel, initially a vocal critic of Anne's looks, proclaims that Anne has turned into a beauty. And Anne's dedicated studying pays off tangibly when she ties Gilbert for first place in the entrance exams.

Anne's progress into adulthood is not always easy, however. She and Diana cling to their childhoods, deciding that they can avoid marriage, children, and adulthood by living together as old maids. The girls know that they will be separated, as Anne will go to college and Diana will not. Their separation at the end of every day, as Anne studies with the Queen's Academy candidates while Diana goes home, foreshadows the greater separation to come the following year, when Anne will attend Queen's Academy full time. Marilla, too, feels the pangs of impending separation, mourning the loss of Anne's childhood and the nearness of her departure for Queen's Academy. Marilla appreciates the companionship and energy Anne brings to Green Gables. As Anne becomes more adult, Matthew and Marilla grow older; Marilla has frequent head and eye aches, and Matthew has heart troubles.

Anne benefits from the strong women who encourage her. Whereas earlier Marilla does not approve of female teachers, she now encourages Anne to make a career of teaching. Miss Stacy provides a model for Anne's possible career as a teacher. Even Mrs. Rachel, who is so often very critical of Anne, takes pride in Anne's academic achievements and begins to respect her as a woman.

The pace of the novel mirrors the pace of Anne's life. Earlier in the novel, each minor event, each cooking accident and social gaffe, fills Anne's mind, and so fills an entire chapter. As Anne matures, the events of her life move more quickly, and she begins to think of important plans like going to college. As a result, the novel's pace accelerates. Instead of focusing on one daylong event, as do the early chapters, these chapters begin to cover entire school years. The acceleration of the narrative does not necessarily suggest that Anne is growing up too quickly; rather, it shows that Anne is maturing and that what she deems important has changed. In her youth she focuses on immediate events, but as she grows older she develops a broader, more far-reaching perspective.

Chapters 33–36

Summary—Chapter 33: The Hotel Concert
Diana, now locally famous for her fashion sense, helps Anne dress for a performance at the upscale White Sands Hotel. Diana suggests a dress of white organdy for Anne's slim figure; Anne can adorn the dress with the string of pearls Matthew recently gave her as a gift.

Anne, accustomed to public speaking, is levelheaded about the affair until she enters the hotel dressing room by herself and is swallowed up in the bustle of elegantly dressed city women. Suddenly, she feels out of place in her simple dress and pearls, which looked lovely in her room at Green Gables but now seem plain next to the other ladies' silks, laces, and diamonds. Onstage, Anne sits between a stout lady who occasionally turns to scrutinize her and a girl in white lace who laughs loudly about the country bumpkins at the affair. The show of wealth and culture intimidates Anne, and stage fright assails her. For several moments, she feels she must run off the stage. Then she sees Gilbert's face in the audience, and the unbearable thought of failing in front of him spurs her on. She delivers a recitation so accomplished that it impresses even the girl in white lace. Afterward, the stout lady, who is the wife of an American millionaire, introduces her to everybody, and she receives many compliments.

On the ride home, Diana tells Anne she overheard a rich American man comment on Anne's hair and face, saying he wanted to paint her. Later, in response to Jane Andrews's wistful observations about all the jewels and riches that were on display, Anne says that she already feels rich in her own skin, with her imagination and the gift of Matthew's string of pearls.

Summary — Chapter 34: A Queen's Girl

> *It won't make a bit of difference where I go or how much I change outwardly; at heart I shall always be your little Anne.*
>
> (See QUOTATIONS, p. 54)

Anne's departure for Queen's Academy is imminent, and everyone at Green Gables helps with the preparations. Marilla changes her ideas about fashion and buys Anne fabric for a fancy evening dress. When Anne tries the dress on and recites a poem for Matthew and Marilla, Marilla begins to cry. At first proud that her poem has moved Marilla, Anne realizes her departure is what makes Marilla sad and reassures her that though she has grown up, she is still the same person, saying, "It won't make a bit of difference where I go or how much I change outwardly; at heart I will always be your little Anne." They embrace, and Matthew reflects that it was Providence (God's will), not luck, that sent Anne to them in the first place.

On the first day at Queen's Academy, Gilbert's presence in the advanced class comforts Anne. Although Anne and Gilbert never speak to each other, his presence reminds her of the rivalry that has motivated her for so many years. Anne is lonely in the classroom full of unfamiliar people and miserable later that night in her room at the boardinghouse. Just as Anne starts crying, Josie Pye shows up, and Anne is delighted to see a familiar face, even though she dislikes Josie. Jane and Ruby visit, and Jane admits that she has been crying too. Josie announces the news of the Avery Scholarship, which provides money for the best student in English to attend a four-year college after his or her one-year program at Queen's Academy. Anne immediately imagines Matthew's pride if she were to earn a bachelor's degree.

SUMMARY—CHAPTER 35: THE WINTER AT QUEEN'S

> *All the Beyond was hers with its possibilities lurking rosily in the oncoming years—each year a rose of promise to be woven into an immortal chaplet.*
> (See QUOTATIONS, p. 55)

Anne's homesickness wears off as the school year progresses. Midway through the year, the scholars at Queen's Academy stop their weekend visits to Avonlea and prepare for exams in the spring. Anne finds that though she is as ambitious as ever, her rivalry with Gilbert has lost some of its power. The thought of defeating him academically still excites her because he is a worthy opponent, but she no longer cares about beating him just to humiliate him. In fact, she secretly wishes to be friends with him. Seeing him walking with Ruby Gillis all the time makes her wonder what Gilbert sees in Ruby, since Ruby has none of the ambition or thoughtfulness that Anne and Gilbert share.

Anne's circle of friends expands as she meets other girls in her class. She also continues her friendship with Aunt Josephine. At the end of the term, while all the other girls are nervous about exams, Anne forgets about the pressure of school and enjoys the beautiful sights of spring.

> *Next to trying and winning, the best thing is trying and failing.* (See QUOTATIONS, p. 56)

SUMMARY—CHAPTER 36: THE GLORY AND THE DREAM
On the morning the exam results are announced, Anne is too nervous to check the list, but someone spots her name and cries that she

has won the Avery Scholarship and Gilbert Blythe the Gold Medal. A swarm of people surrounds Anne and congratulates her, and when Matthew and Marilla come to the Queen's Academy for commencement, they can hardly contain their pride in Anne's achievements. Anne goes back to Green Gables after commencement, rejoicing in all the familiar sights and in spending time with Diana. Anne plans to continue her education at Redmond College in the fall, while Jane and Ruby will begin to teach. She learns from Diana that Gilbert will be teaching also, since his father cannot afford to send him to Redmond, which disappoints Anne.

At Green Gables, Anne and Marilla discuss the shaky position of Abbey Bank, where the Cuthberts have always kept their money. Rumors of the bank's trouble have persuaded Marilla to ask Matthew about moving their money, but he has reassured her that the bank is all right. Anne notices that Marilla and Matthew are not looking well. Marilla says that her headaches have become severe and her deteriorating vision has made sewing and reading uncomfortable. Matthew has been having heart trouble all spring but cannot bring himself to follow the doctor's order to rest more.

Analysis — Chapters 33–36

Although Anne has always fantasized about material wealth, fancy jewels, and fine dresses, she has never been overly materialistic or obsessed with acquiring nice possessions. The world of wealth and culture she sees at the White Sands Hotel does not appeal to her as much as her simple life in Green Gables, which is rich in natural beauty, love, and imagination. During Anne's childhood, Marilla and Mrs. Rachel warn Anne frequently that lofty dreams, especially dreams of wealth, will lead only to disappointment. But Anne is not disappointed when riches do not measure up to her dreams. After indulging in dreams of opulence as a child, she now calmly realizes the worth of her simple, happy life.

As an adult, Anne dreams not of riches and of golden hair, but of academic and professional success. The word "ambition" appears nearly as often in the later chapters as the word "imagination" does in the early ones, showing how Anne's character has changed. In some ways, however, Anne can cast aside her childhood dreams because they have all come true. The red hair she so loathes as a youngster has turned a rich auburn color. She claims earlier that she would rather be pretty than smart, and now she is both pretty and smart. She earlier wants to be well behaved, and she now comports herself with compassion and maturity as well as good manners.

Anne's ideas about success change, and she ceases to define success as beating Gilbert Blythe. She even says, "Next to trying and winning, the best thing is trying and failing." Whereas earlier she thinks that she would rather fail the entrance exam than be beaten by Gilbert, now she does not equate success with winning. When she feels she cannot recite her poem at the White Sands Hotel, she considers leaving the stage, but decides it is better to recite the poem and be humiliated than not to try at all. This newfound belief that losing to another person is not as humiliating as not trying to succeed is a sign of her growing maturity.

Anne's feelings for Gilbert gradually change too. She thinks of their rivalry with affection and nostalgia, and is disappointed to learn that he will not go with her to Redmond College. She is now able to see that they share many character traits and might have been close friends were it not for her own competitiveness. Anne has not completely outgrown her childish traits, however, and the stubbornness that created the rift in the first place still prevents her from forging a friendship with Gilbert.

Chapters 37–38

Summary — Chapter 37:
The Reaper Whose Name Is Death

Marilla sees Matthew's gray, sad face and calls to him sharply. At that moment, Anne sees him collapse at the threshold of Green Gables. Marilla and Anne try to revive him, but he dies instantly of a shock-induced heart attack. The shock came from reading a notice that Abbey Bank, where the Cuthberts keep all their money, has failed. For the first time, Matthew becomes the center of Avonlea's attention as friends visit and run errands for Marilla and Anne. Marilla grieves with impassioned sobs, but Anne cannot muster tears that first day and suffers from a dull inner ache. Marilla hears her weeping in the middle of the night and goes to comfort her. In a rare moment of spoken affection, Marilla tells Anne that despite her own harsh ways, she loves Anne and cannot imagine life without her.

When the pain of Matthew's death becomes less immediate, Anne finds herself enjoying her friends' company and life at Green

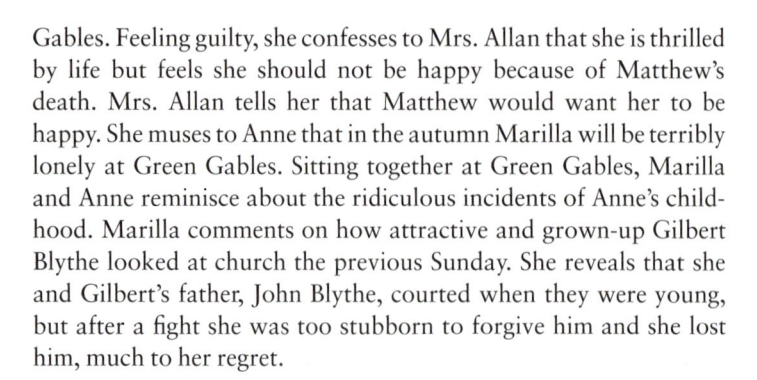

Gables. Feeling guilty, she confesses to Mrs. Allan that she is thrilled by life but feels she should not be happy because of Matthew's death. Mrs. Allan tells her that Matthew would want her to be happy. She muses to Anne that in the autumn Marilla will be terribly lonely at Green Gables. Sitting together at Green Gables, Marilla and Anne reminisce about the ridiculous incidents of Anne's childhood. Marilla comments on how attractive and grown-up Gilbert Blythe looked at church the previous Sunday. She reveals that she and Gilbert's father, John Blythe, courted when they were young, but after a fight she was too stubborn to forgive him and she lost him, much to her regret.

Summary—Chapter 38: The Bend in the Road

> *When I left Queen's my future seemed to stretch out before me like a straight road.... Now there is a bend in it.... It has a fascination of its own, that bend.*
> (See QUOTATIONS, p. 57)

Marilla goes to town to see a visiting eye doctor and returns with bad news: she must give up reading, sewing, and crying, or else she will go blind. That night, Anne reflects on all that has happened since her return from Queen's Academy. She decides that she will stay at Green Gables to take care of Marilla rather than accept the Avery Scholarship, and once her mind is set, she finds comfort in her path of duty. A few days later, Anne learns that Marilla is considering selling Green Gables, since she will be unable to maintain it alone. Anne tells Marilla that she will stay at Green Gables and teach at a school called Carmody, since the Avonlea school post has already been assigned to Gilbert. Later, Mrs. Rachel informs her that Gilbert has gone to the Avonlea trustees and asked that the Avonlea post be given to Anne so that she can be closer to Marilla—a sacrifice that means Gilbert must teach at White Sands and pay for boarding. Anne is elated, knowing that she can live at home, comfort Marilla, and see Diana often. When she runs into Gilbert later, she breaks their tradition of silence to thank him for his generosity. She extends her hand, which he takes eagerly, and they begin the close friendship they have both wanted.

Analysis—Chapters 37–38

Anne struggles to understand Matthew's death, her first real experience with losing a loved one. She has had experiences with death before: her biological parents died when she was a baby, and both of her foster fathers died. But Anne does not remember her parents or their deaths and was not close to her foster parents. Up until now, she has romanticized death and created stories about lovers and tragic endings; death has not been real for her, but a topic of fantasy. Now that Matthew is gone, Anne understands what it is to lose someone she loves, and she grieves. Although at first Anne cannot reconcile her feelings of grief with her continued pleasure in life, she eventually comes to accept these apparently contradictory feelings as part of a natural response to tragedy. Coming to understand death marks another step on Anne's path to adulthood.

The death of Matthew and the decay of Marilla's health cause Anne and Marilla to reverse roles. Anne's adulthood begins with her decision to take care of the woman who has taken care of her since Anne was a child. As a young girl, Anne and her friends define adulthood as the age when a girl may have a beau or wear her hair up. Now, Anne understands that adulthood involves not superficialities but the assumption of responsibilities.

Anne's willingness to begin a friendship with Gilbert also marks her maturity. Although Marilla does not moralize to Anne, she tells her a story that makes a clear point: she lost the man she loved, John Blythe, because of her Anne-like stubbornness, and years of loneliness and regret ensued. The fact that Marilla tells Anne this story illustrates the trust Marilla places in Anne. Marilla is a reserved, usually unemotional woman, but she manages to tell this painful story to Anne because she loves her so much. The story also suggests that Marilla now sees Anne not as a child but as a woman and a confidante who will understand delicate matters. Finally, it explains some of Marilla's behavior. She is not sexless and cold, as she first appears; rather, she lives in the same town with the man she loved and lost and must bear her regrets and loneliness with fortitude that sometimes looks like ice. Because Anne understands the implications of the story and because she feels real gratitude for Gilbert's sacrifice, she finds it in herself to forgive him.

Important Quotations Explained

1. "Isn't it splendid to think of all the things there are to find out about? It just makes me feel glad to be alive—it's such an interesting world. It wouldn't be half so interesting if we knew all about everything, would it? There'd be no scope for imagination then, would there?"

Anne speaks these words to Matthew in Chapter 2 as they ride from the train station to Green Gables. Their first real conversation consists of Anne's optimistic, inventive musings and Matthew's shy, one-word answers. Nevertheless, a kinship springs up between the two, and Anne's rambling speeches spark Matthew's interest. He finds Anne full of curiosity and imagination. His own world has been a quiet and dull one, and Anne sweeps a refreshing breath of life into his staid existence. This quotation typifies Anne's attitude. She wants to find out about the world, and she sees potential difficulties, like the massive amount she does not know, as happy challenges. Imagination is central to Anne's existence. She takes pride and refuge in her own imagination, and wants others to imagine too.

2. "I'm not a bit changed—not really. I'm only just pruned down and branched out. The real me—back here—is just the same. It won't make a bit of difference where I go or how much I change outwardly; at heart I shall always be your little Anne, who will love you and Matthew and dear Green Gables more and better every day of her life."

Anne expresses these thoughts in Chapter 34, before she is to leave for Queen's Academy. In a novel centered around Anne's evolution, this quotation at first seems surprising, for here Anne expresses her lack of change. Although Anne has changed remarkably, she likens herself to a tree in order to assure Marilla that although her branches may grow, at her roots she will remain the same, firmly ensconced in her home and family. Here Anne uses a metaphor drawn from nature, her constant source of comfort in difficult times. The fact that Anne feels the need to make this speech at all points to the changes that her presence has wrought in Marilla. Anne's affectionate gestures and loving speeches have tempered Marilla's buttoned-up severity so much that Marilla now weeps openly at the thought of Anne's departure. In one sense, the fact that Anne must reassure the saddened Marilla is a happy event, for the cause of the speech shows Marilla's great love for her adopted daughter.

3. All the Beyond was hers with its possibilities lurking rosily in the oncoming years—each year a rose of promise to be woven into an immortal chaplet.

This sentence from Chapter 35 describes Anne's feelings about the future. Anne has made a great success of herself at college and imagines her triumphant future. One of Anne's enduring and endearing traits is her eternal optimism. Even as an orphan whom no one loves before she comes to Green Gables, she maintains a positive outlook on life, eager for experience.

This quotation uses imagery from nature to create a link between nature and imagination. Anne is very fond of nature, which has always been a source of comfort to her. Though she has matured and is thinking about the future, she reveals the lingering vestiges of her childhood sentimentality.

4. Next to trying and winning, the best thing is trying and failing.

Anne expresses this opinion in Chapter 35, as she prepares for her exams at Queen's Academy. Earlier in the novel, Anne thinks that success is beating everyone else and humiliating her rival Gilbert Blythe in the process. She would rather fail utterly than come in second place behind Gilbert. This definition of success motivates Anne, inspiring her to work hard in school for the pleasure of triumphing over Gilbert. Once Anne is at college, however, her definition of success begins to shift. She comes to think affectionately of her rivalry with Gilbert, and although she still enjoys the competition, she wants to win for herself, not for the pleasure of seeing Gilbert embarrassed. She performs onstage at the White Sands Hotel despite her terrible nervousness, because she feels that to fail to try is far more humiliating than to try and fail. She also performs because she sees Gilbert in the audience. It seems she cannot bear to fail in front of him because she does not want to disappoint her worthy opponent.

5. "When I left Queen's my future seemed to stretch out before me like a straight road. I thought I could see along it for many a milestone. Now there is a bend in it. I don't know what lies around the bend, but I'm going to believe that the best does. It has a fascination of its own, that bend."

Anne expresses these thoughts in Chapter 38 after deciding to give up the prestigious Avery Scholarship in order to care for Marilla at home. This quotation communicates one of Anne's defining characteristics: optimism in the face of uncertainty. In this case, optimism is no easy feat. In order to do the right thing, Anne must give up some of her ambitions. Anne uses slightly overblown, sentimental language to describe her prospects after commencement, talking of roses and chaplets and immortality. Here, however, she sounds more sensible and realistic. She knows she will not achieve great things by staying at home and providing loving care for Marilla, but she finds real happiness in the knowledge that she is doing the right thing. Instead of immortal roses, she now thinks of a simple, if mysterious, road. Roads are significant throughout the novel; when Anne first arrives in Avonlea, she rapturously renames the road into town "The White Way of Delight." Both then and now, she rides hopefully along a road to an unknown future.

Key Facts

FULL TITLE
Anne of Green Gables

AUTHOR
Lucy Maud Montgomery

TYPE OF WORK
Novel

GENRE
Coming-of-age novel; juvenile literature

LANGUAGE
English

TIME AND PLACE WRITTEN
1908; Canada

DATE OF FIRST PUBLICATION
1908

PUBLISHER
L. C. Page

NARRATOR
The narrator relates the events of the novel in the third person and has access to every character's thoughts and emotions. Biased and partial, the narrator often mocks, condemns, or shows affection for the characters.

POINT OF VIEW
The novel is written mainly from Anne's point of view, but it frequently switches to Marilla's and sometimes to Matthew's points of view.

TONE
The narrator is affectionate toward Anne, satirical when describing small-town life, and sentimental and gushing when describing nature.

TENSE
Past

SETTING (TIME)
The turn of the twentieth century

SETTING (PLACE)
Prince Edward Island, Canada

PROTAGONIST
Anne Shirley

MAJOR CONFLICT
Anne struggles to reconcile her imagination and romantic notions with the rigid expectations of traditional Avonlea society.

RISING ACTION
Anne's continuous mistakes in her domestic duties and social interactions

CLIMAX
Matthew's death and Anne's success at college

FALLING ACTION
Anne's decision to stay at Green Gables and teach in Avonlea

THEMES
The conflict between imagination and expectation; sentimentality versus emotion

MOTIFS
Fashion; images of nature

SYMBOLS
Anne's red hair; the light from Diana's window

FORESHADOWING
Anne's dream about having a best friend hints at the close relationship she develops with Diana Barry; Matthew's heart trouble foreshadows his death at the end of the novel, just as Marilla's headaches foreshadow her health problems.

Study Questions & Essay Topics

Study Questions

1. *Good behavior is a subject that troubles Anne. Choose two main characters from the novel and discuss the different ways each character approaches the problem of being good.*

Upon her arrival at Green Gables, Anne immediately comes into conflict with the people of Avonlea, especially Marilla, because of their different conceptions of what it means to be good. Marilla follows a strict definition of good behavior based on traditional roles and propriety, and she uses behavior to judge a person's underlying moral character. To Marilla, Anne's ignorance of the proper way to pray suggests that Anne is not only badly brought up but possibly wicked. When Anne decorates her hat with wildflowers on the way to church, she unwittingly draws stares and laughter from established churchgoers. Marilla feels that such Anne's actions reflect badly on her. Although Marilla understands and sympathizes with Anne's lack of formal education, she believes that standard rules of behavior should govern a young girl's actions.

Anne is perplexed by the new moral codes she encounters while living with Marilla. She includes several personal wishes in her first prayer, asking that God make her pretty and change her red hair, which suggests that Anne thinks of prayer as an opportunity to express her fondest desires. Similarly, she does not understand why wearing flowers to church is objectionable, as the other girls wear artificial flowers in their hats. Expectations that conflict with her own common sense confuse Anne. Anne believes that if good intentions drive a person, it does not matter if her actions are unusual, because that person is still inherently good.

As Anne matures and Marilla mellows, their conflict over the definition of good behavior becomes less strident. At the beginning of her stay, Anne thinks that if she feels justified in her actions, it is right for her to act in any way she chooses. For example, Anne attacks Mrs. Rachel when Mrs. Rachel makes a derogatory remark about Anne's red hair. Although Marilla sympathizes with Anne's feelings, she insists that Anne follow the accepted code of conduct. Eventually, Anne comes to appreciate pleasant behavior and treating others with kindness and respect. She maintains her independent spirit, but begins to understand the importance of good behavior as a way of getting along with people and that acting as expected puts people at ease.

2. *How do Anne's conceptions of the future evolve throughout the novel?*

As an unloved orphan, Anne cultivates the ability to imagine exciting futures. She constructs futures for herself based on imaginative, romantic notions of beauty, eternal love, and tragic loss. When Anne arrives at Green Gables, she dreams of a future in which she is named Lady Cordelia and has a best friend, a home, and people who love her. She imagines that her red hair will disappear and that riches will surround her. When some of these dreams come true, they disappoint or please her to varying degrees. She loves her home and her family, but her dreams of riches fall flat. When she and Diana visit Aunt Josephine in the city, for example, partaking of her wealthy lifestyle, Anne discovers that the fantasy of wealth gives her more pleasure than the fact of wealth.

As Anne matures, she envisions her future differently. Her romanticism fades, and she regards her childhood fantasies as undesirable. Ambition replaces romanticism, and Anne strives to achieve real goals. She studies and works with the same zeal that she earlier applies to daydreaming. At the end of the novel, Anne's vision of her future draws on her romantic notions as well as her ambition. Anne gives up her unrealistic dream of becoming rich and spoiled and her realistic dream of attending a four-year college. She settles for a future that combines her idealism and her work ethic. She will stay in her well-loved Avonlea, with the house and family she dreamed of as a child. She will continue her studies and teach at the school, but she will also fulfill her duties as a responsible adult by caring for the ones who love her.

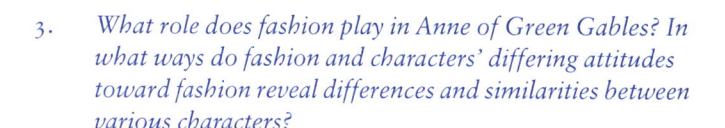

3. *What role does fashion play in Anne of Green Gables? In what ways do fashion and characters' differing attitudes toward fashion reveal differences and similarities between various characters?*

As a child, Anne dreams of wearing fancy dresses and puffed sleeves, but Marilla, always sensible, considers interest in fashion an expression of vanity. Marilla believes that an upstanding Christian woman should condemn fashion. The conflict between Marilla's and Anne's attitudes toward dress reflects broader differences in their personalities and beliefs. Anne often equates morality with physical appearance, saying that it would be easier to be good if only she were pretty and well dressed. Marilla, on the other hand, considers morality to exclude concern with dress.

Matthew's timid entry into the realm of women's fashion is the turning point in Anne and Marilla's conflict. Although Matthew is normally unaware of feminine pursuits, he notices that Anne stands apart from her friends because of her plain, unfashionable clothes. He decides to get Anne a new dress and courageously faces a female store clerk in town, marking an important change in his character. Fashion is a means by which Matthew shows his evolution as a character. For love of Anne, he becomes a bit more brave.

Matthew's purchase of a dress for Anne changes both Marilla's and Anne's attitudes. Marilla sees that Anne is the same person in a plain dress or in a fancy one. Marilla no longer relies solely on dogma for moral guidance but is willing to accept new ideas. Anne realizes that her physical appearance does not inform her morality and that she can be a good person no matter what she wears. Anne learns that beauty is more than just wearing a dress with puffed sleeves and that behavior, not fashion, makes a person good.

Suggested Essay Topics

1. Discuss the role of imagination in the novel. How does it drive plot events, and how do characters' imaginations evolve throughout the novel?

2. Discuss the various ways loss and separation appear in the novel. How does Anne's conception of loss change at the end of the novel?

3. How does Anne's character change, and how does her character change those around her?

4. Why are confessions important in *Anne of Green Gables*? Compare Anne's confessions and discuss how each one has a different impact on her.

5. How does Marilla's character change as a result of Anne's arrival at Green Gables?

Review & Resources

Quiz

1. Why does Anne break a slate over Gilbert's head?

    A. He makes fun of her nose
    B. He makes fun of her hair
    C. She means to hit Mr. Phillips but slips
    D. She is jealous that he is courting Diana

2. What is the name of Diana's home?

    A. Dryad's Bubble
    B. Birch Park
    C. Orchard Slope
    D. Verdant Hills

3. Why does Anne give up her scholarship?

    A. She falls in love with Gilbert
    B. She can't bear to be apart from Diana
    C. She feels guilty for cheating on the qualifying exam
    D. She wants to stay home and take care of Marilla

4. Whose life does Anne save?

    A. Gilbert Blythe's
    B. Minnie May's
    C. Diana's
    D. Ruby Gillis's

5. On the day of Anne's arrival, why is Marilla hesitant to keep Anne?

    A. Marilla wants a boy to work the farm
    B. Anne talks too much
    C. Anne is rude to Mrs. Rachel
    D. Marilla doubts her ability to raise a child

6. What is Anne's favorite fashion trend?

   A. Lace and ribbon
   B. White petticoats
   C. Pink bonnets
   D. Puffed sleeves

7. What catastrophe occurs when the Allans come to tea?

   A. Anne puts liniment in the cake
   B. Anne announces that a mouse has drowned in the plum-pudding sauce
   C. Anne sets a houseplant on fire
   D. Anne breaks her ankle

8. Which fellow classmate do Anne and Diana dislike?

   A. Jane Andrews
   B. Josie Pye
   C. Ruby Gillis
   D. Charlie Sloane

9. Why is Marilla dismayed by Anne's apology to Mrs. Rachel?

   A. Anne stains her dress as she is apologizing
   B. Mrs. Rachel refuses to accept the apology
   C. Anne seems to enjoy making the apology
   D. Matthew interrupts to ask about buying hayseed

10. The day of the picnic, Anne is forced to make a false confession about which of the following?

    A. Losing Marilla's brooch
    B. Sneaking to Diana's house late at night
    C. Breaking a slate over Gilbert's head
    D. Lying to Matthew

11. Why does Anne become terrified to make night journeys to Diana's house?

    A. She learns the legend of the Avonlea murderer
    B. She thinks Diana's mother will yell at her
    C. She imagines that the woods are haunted
    D. She is afraid she will run into Gilbert

12. In which of the following situations does Gilbert find Anne?

   A. Stuck up a tree
   B. With her dress caught on the train track
   C. Being beat up by some girls
   D. Clinging to a bridge pile

13. How does Anne break her ankle?

   A. Tripping over a hole in the ground
   B. Falling off the Barrys' roof
   C. Fighting with Josie Pye
   D. Running through the woods to the Barry house

14. Why does Aunt Josephine threaten to take away Diana's music lessons?

   A. Diana and Anne jump on her in the middle of the night
   B. Diana has an overactive imagination
   C. Anne tries to poison Minnie May
   D. Diana gets a bad grade on a spelling test

15. Why does Mrs. Barry refuse to let Diana play with Anne?

   A. Anne looks ridiculous in church
   B. Mrs. Barry has fallen ill and needs Diana around the house
   C. Anne gets Diana drunk
   D. Mrs. Barry and Marilla have been lifelong rivals

16. Why does Marilla cut Anne's hair?

   A. As punishment for being wicked
   B. Anne gets gum caught in it
   C. Marilla insists that Anne have a stylish hairdo
   D. Anne dyes her hair green

17. Why does Anne stay after school with Miss Stacy every day?

    A. To prepare for the Queen's Academy entrance exam
    B. To get extra help in geometry
    C. As punishment for reading a novel during class
    D. Because they gossip together about the other students

18. What does Mrs. Rachel think about women teachers?

    A. She thinks they should teach only female students
    B. She thinks teaching is not an appropriate job for a woman
    C. She wishes she had had a woman teacher
    D. She hates all teachers, regardless of gender

19. Why does Matthew balk when he goes to buy Anne's new dress?

    A. He does not have enough money to pay for the dress
    B. He does not like the store's clothing selection
    C. There is a woman clerk in the store
    D. He decides that Marilla can make just as good a dress as the ones in the store

20. What is Matthew and Marilla's relationship?

    A. They are married
    B. They are siblings
    C. They are cousins
    D. They are father and daughter

21. Where will Anne begin teaching?

    A. Avonlea
    B. White Sands
    C. Charlottetown
    D. Carmody

22. What is the name of the woman who takes custody of Anne so that Anne will help with her three sets of twins?

    A. Mrs. Spencer
    B. Mrs. Andrews
    C. Mrs. Allan
    D. Mrs. Hammond

23. What helps Anne recover from her stage fright at the White Sands Hotel?

    A. The stout lady's jokes
    B. The sight of Gilbert's face
    C. Diana's applause
    D. Mrs. Allan's kind words

24. While studying at Queen's Academy, where does Anne live?

    A. In a boardinghouse
    B. At Green Gables
    C. At Redmond College
    D. At Aunt Josephine's mansion

25. What shock causes Matthew's heart attack?

    A. Seeing Anne all grown up
    B. Running into Mr. Blythe, whom he hates
    C. Learning that Anne is going away to college
    D. Learning that Abbey Bank has failed

Answer Key:

1: B; 2: C; 3: D; 4: B; 5: A; 6: D; 7: A; 8: B; 9: C; 10: A; 11: C; 12: D; 13: B; 14: A; 15: C; 16: D; 17: A; 18: B; 19: C; 20: B; 21: A; 22: D; 23: B; 24: A; 25: D

SUGGESTIONS FOR FURTHER READING

BRUCE, HARRY. *Maud: The Life of L. M. Montgomery.* New York: Seal Bantam Books, 1992.

MONTGOMERY, L. M. *Anne of Avonlea.* New York: Bantam Books, 1987.

———. *Anne of Ingleside.* New York: Bantam Books, 1987.

———. *Anne of the Island.* New York: Bantam Books, 1987.

———. *Anne of Windy Poplars.* New York: Bantam Books, 1987.

———. *Anne's House of Dreams.* New York: Bantam Books, 1987.

———. *Emily of New Moon.* New York: Bantam Books, 1983.

———. *Rainbow Valley.* New York: Bantam Books, 1987.

———. *Rilla of Ingleside.* New York: Bantam Books, 1987.

A Note on the Type

The typeface used in SparkNotes study guides is Sabon, created by master typographer Jan Tschichold in 1964. Tschichold revolutionized the field of graphic design twice: first with his use of asymmetrical layouts and sanserif type in the 1930s when he was affiliated with the Bauhaus, then by abandoning assymetry and calling for a return to the classic ideals of design. Sabon, his only extant typeface, is emblematic of his latter program: Tschichold's design is a recreation of the types made by Claude Garamond, the great French typographer of the Renaissance, and his contemporary Robert Granjon. Fittingly, it is named for Garamond's apprentice, Jacques Sabon.

SparkNotes Test Preparation Guides

The SparkNotes team figured it was time to cut standardized tests down to size. We've studied the tests for you, so that SparkNotes test prep guides are:

Smarter:
Packed with critical-thinking skills and test-taking strategies that will improve your score.

Better:
Fully up to date, covering all new features of the tests, with study tips on every type of question.

Faster:
Our books cover exactly what you need to know for the test. No more, no less.

SparkNotes Guide to the SAT & PSAT
SparkNotes Guide to the SAT & PSAT—Deluxe Internet Edition
SparkNotes Guide to the ACT
SparkNotes Guide to the ACT—Deluxe Internet Edition
SparkNotes Guide to the SAT II Writing
SparkNotes Guide to the SAT II U.S. History
SparkNotes Guide to the SAT II Math Ic
SparkNotes Guide to the SAT II Math IIc
SparkNotes Guide to the SAT II Biology
SparkNotes Guide to the SAT II Physics

SAT and PSAT are registered trademarks of the College Entrance Examination Board, which does not endorse these books.
ACT is a registered trademark of ACT, Inc. which neither sponsors nor endorses these books.

SparkNotes Study Guides:

1984
The Adventures of Huckleberry Finn
The Adventures of Tom Sawyer
The Aeneid
All Quiet on the Western Front
And Then There Were None
Angela's Ashes
Animal Farm
Anne of Green Gables
Antony and Cleopatra
As I Lay Dying
As You Like It
The Awakening
The Bean Trees
The Bell Jar
Beloved
Beowulf
Billy Budd
Black Boy
Bless Me, Ultima
The Bluest Eye
Brave New World
The Brothers Karamazov
The Call of the Wild
Candide
The Canterbury Tales
Catch-22
The Catcher in the Rye
The Chosen
Cold Mountain
Cold Sassy Tree
The Color Purple
The Count of Monte Cristo
Crime and Punishment
The Crucible
Cry, the Beloved Country
Cyrano de Bergerac
Death of a Salesman
The Diary of a Young Girl
Doctor Faustus
A Doll's House
Don Quixote
Dr. Jekyll and Mr. Hyde
Dracula
Dune
Emma
Ethan Frome
Fahrenheit 451
Fallen Angels
A Farewell to Arms
Flowers for Algernon
The Fountainhead
Frankenstein
The Glass Menagerie
Gone With the Wind
The Good Earth
The Grapes of Wrath
Great Expectations
The Great Gatsby
Gulliver's Travels
Hamlet
The Handmaid's Tale
Hard Times
Harry Potter and the Sorcerer's Stone
Heart of Darkness
Henry IV, Part I
Henry V
Hiroshima
The Hobbit
The House of the Seven Gables
I Know Why the Caged Bird Sings
The Iliad
Inferno
Invisible Man
Jane Eyre
Johnny Tremain
The Joy Luck Club
Julius Caesar
The Jungle
The Killer Angels
King Lear
The Last of the Mohicans
Les Misérables
A Lesson Before Dying
The Little Prince
Little Women
Lord of the Flies
Macbeth
Madame Bovary
A Man for All Seasons
The Mayor of Casterbridge
The Merchant of Venice
A Midsummer Night's Dream
Moby-Dick
Much Ado About Nothing
My Ántonia
Mythology
Native Son
The New Testament
Night
The Odyssey
The Oedipus Trilogy
Of Mice and Men
The Old Man and the Sea
The Old Testament
Oliver Twist
The Once and Future King
One Flew Over the Cuckoo's Nest
One Hundred Years of Solitude
Othello
Our Town
The Outsiders
Paradise Lost
The Pearl
The Picture of Dorian Gray
A Portrait of the Artist as a Young Man
Pride and Prejudice
The Prince
A Raisin in the Sun
The Red Badge of Courage
The Republic
Richard III
Robinson Crusoe
Romeo and Juliet
The Scarlet Letter
A Separate Peace
Silas Marner
Sir Gawain and the Green Knight
Slaughterhouse-Five
Snow Falling on Cedars
The Sound and the Fury
Steppenwolf
The Stranger
A Streetcar Named Desire
The Sun Also Rises
A Tale of Two Cities
The Taming of the Shrew
The Tempest
Tess of the d'Urbervilles
Their Eyes Were Watching God
Things Fall Apart
To Kill a Mockingbird
To the Lighthouse
Treasure Island
Twelfth Night
Ulysses
Uncle Tom's Cabin
Walden
Wuthering Heights
A Yellow Raft in Blue Water